ON THE EDGE

A SOLO HIKER'S JOURNEY

ON THE EDGE

STACIE J. OURLIAN

Stacie Ourlian (signature)

AMBASSADOR INTERNATIONAL
GREENVILLE, SOUTH CAROLINA & BELFAST, NORTHERN IRELAND

www.ambassador-international.com

On the Edge
A Solo Hiker's Journey

© 2015 by Stacie J. Ourlian
All rights reserved

ISBN: 978-1-62020-293-7
eISBN: 978-1-62020-398-9

Scripture quotations taken from THE HOLY BIBLE, NEW INTERNATIONAL VERSION®, NIV® Copyright © 1973, 1978, 1984, 2011 by Biblica, Inc.® Used by permission. All rights reserved worldwide.

Cover Design & Page Layout by Hannah Nichols
EBook Conversion by Anna Raats
Photography by Stacie J. Ourlian

AMBASSADOR INTERNATIONAL
Emerald House
427 Wade Hampton Blvd.
Greenville, SC 29609, USA
www.ambassador-international.com

AMBASSADOR BOOKS
The Mount
2 Woodstock Link
Belfast, BT6 8DD, Northern Ireland, UK
www.ambassadormedia.co.uk

The colophon is a trademark of Ambassador

Dedicated to the One who has helped me understand that life is a precious gift that's worth one hundred percent effort, every day. Thank You, Jesus, for showing me the way through people, through experiences, and through faith. May all people come to know Your holy name and find peace in knowing You are always here, listening and ready to teach.

ACKNOWLEDGEMENTS

I feel blessed to have the opportunity to acknowledge those who have made this book possible. First and foremost, thank you to my mother, Sherry Hershey, for taking time to read my one-page stories when I was eight years old. Thank you for encouraging me and believing that I would, one day, become a published author. Also to my sister, Stephanie Krupinski, for emotional support and encouraging me to be the best person I can be. Thank you to my nieces and nephews for reminding me how great life can be!

Thank you to my eighth-grade English teacher, Sandy Yonker. When I was thirteen years old, I gave you one of my chapter books to read. You took it home and read it in your spare time. You not only edited the entire story, but you also taught me to put detail and description in everything I wrote. Thank you for your words of encouragement and helping me become a better writer.

Thank you to my aunt, Karen Riggan, for giving me a blank journal when I was ten years old. On the inside of the cover you had written, "For you to write all your stories, then I can say I knew you when...." I held on to the journal, determined to prove you right and feeling encouraged by your words.

I feel blessed to have met so many people who have helped me become a stronger Christian. Bonnie Sorter, thank you for helping me create a close relationship with God and find a church. Thank you for your advice and helping me get through the difficult parts of life. Pastor Ron Schultz, thank you for furthering my education in Christ and sending me on the Christian retreat. Thank you for meeting with me over coffee and providing support that I needed. Pastor Mark Witte, thank you for providing me with the basic Christian faith, which allowed me to become a member of Grace Lutheran. Thank you for discussing the Bible with me on the phone and helping further my understanding.

Thank you to Ambassador International for choosing to publish this book and to my editor, Brenda Covert, for helping form it into a masterpiece I will cherish for the rest of my life.

Thank you to all the people whom I mention at the beginning of the book. Without the trials and tribulations I've gone through in the last four years, I don't know that I would have actively sought a relationship with God. I wouldn't change the past for anything in the world because I found God by going through it.

Most importantly, thank You, God, for loving me. Thank You for continuously watching over me, comforting me, encouraging me, and providing for me. Thank You for everything I've experienced in life, good and bad, because through it all, I found You. Continue to guide me every single second of the day so that I'm always going down a path of righteousness and truth. Thank You, God, for the beautiful mountains of Sedona and allowing me the chance to see part of the beauty You've created. Thank You for allowing me to be able to hike and giving me the gift to write. Most of all, thank You for this experience and for the amazing people You put in my path. To God be the glory!

CONTENTS

CHAPTER 1
EVERYTHING IS MEANINGLESS   29

CHAPTER 2
WHERE'S MY MAP?   49

CHAPTER 3
LEFT OR RIGHT?   75

CHAPTER 4
STOP FOR DIRECTIONS   95

CHAPTER 5
EXPECTATIONS OF THE FUTURE   113

CHAPTER 6
THE RACE TO JUDGMENT   127

CHAPTER 7
REACHING THE TOP   141

PHOTOGRAPHY INDEX   153

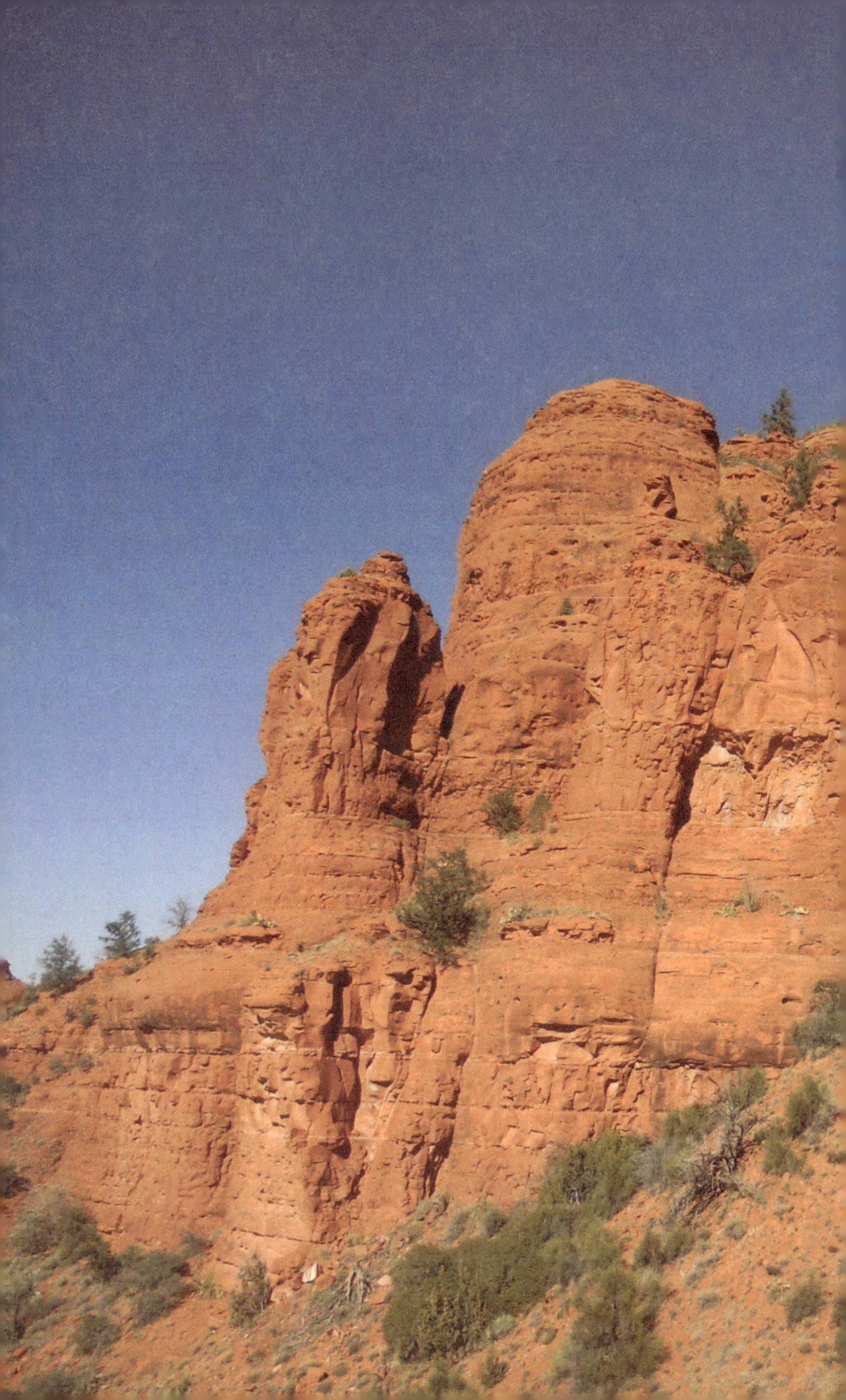

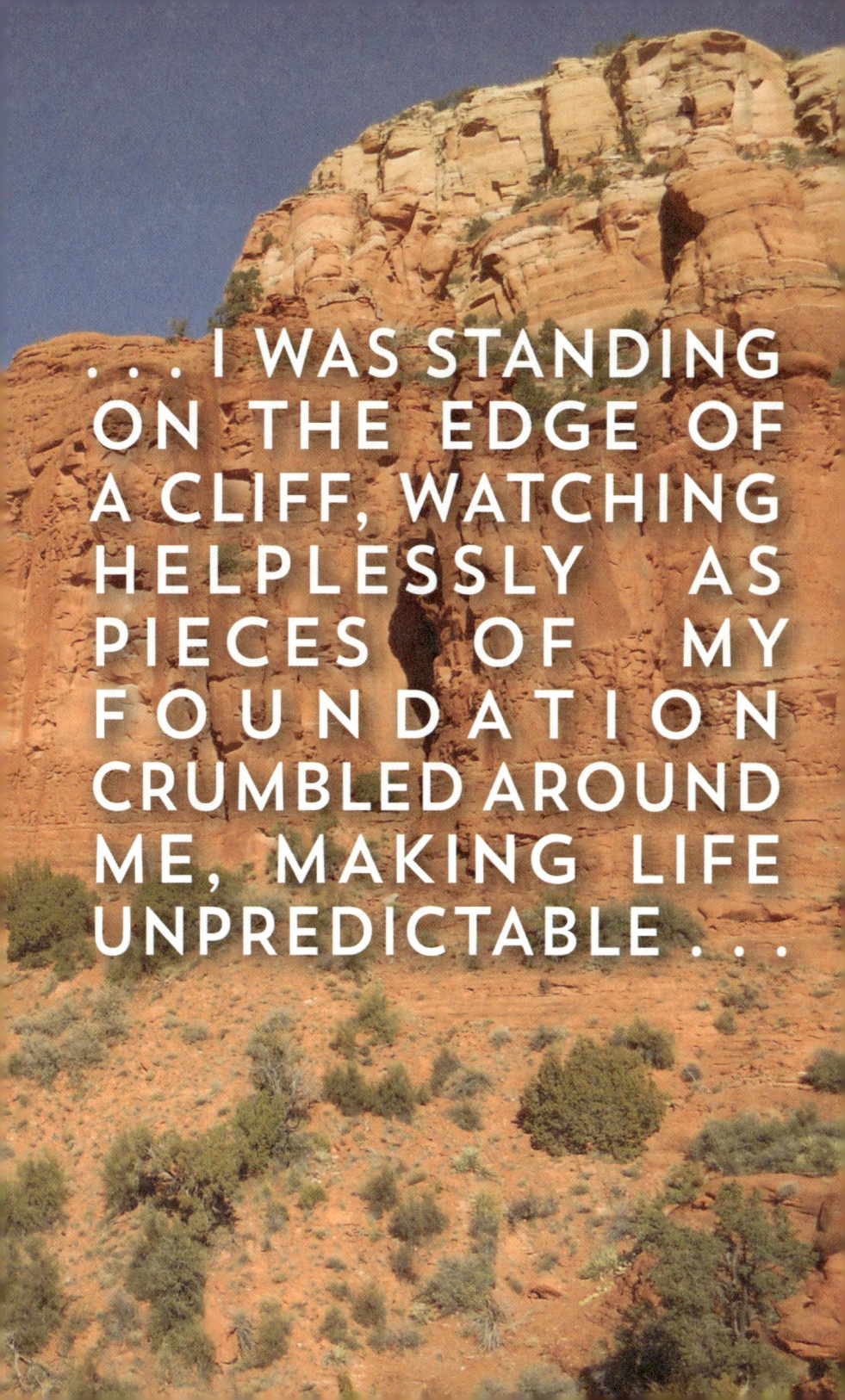

. . . I WAS STANDING ON THE EDGE OF A CLIFF, WATCHING HELPLESSLY AS PIECES OF MY FOUNDATION CRUMBLED AROUND ME, MAKING LIFE UNPREDICTABLE . . .

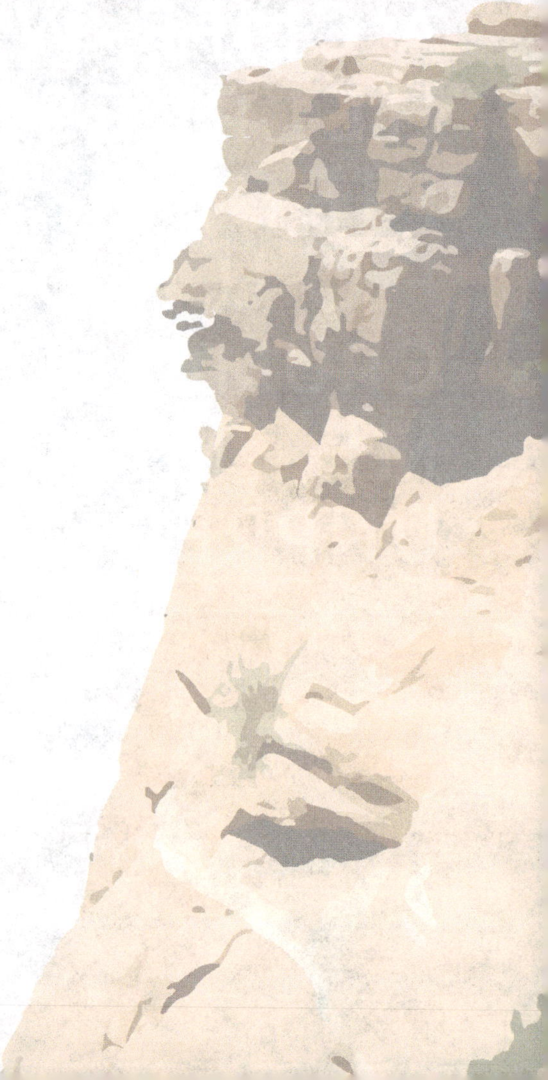

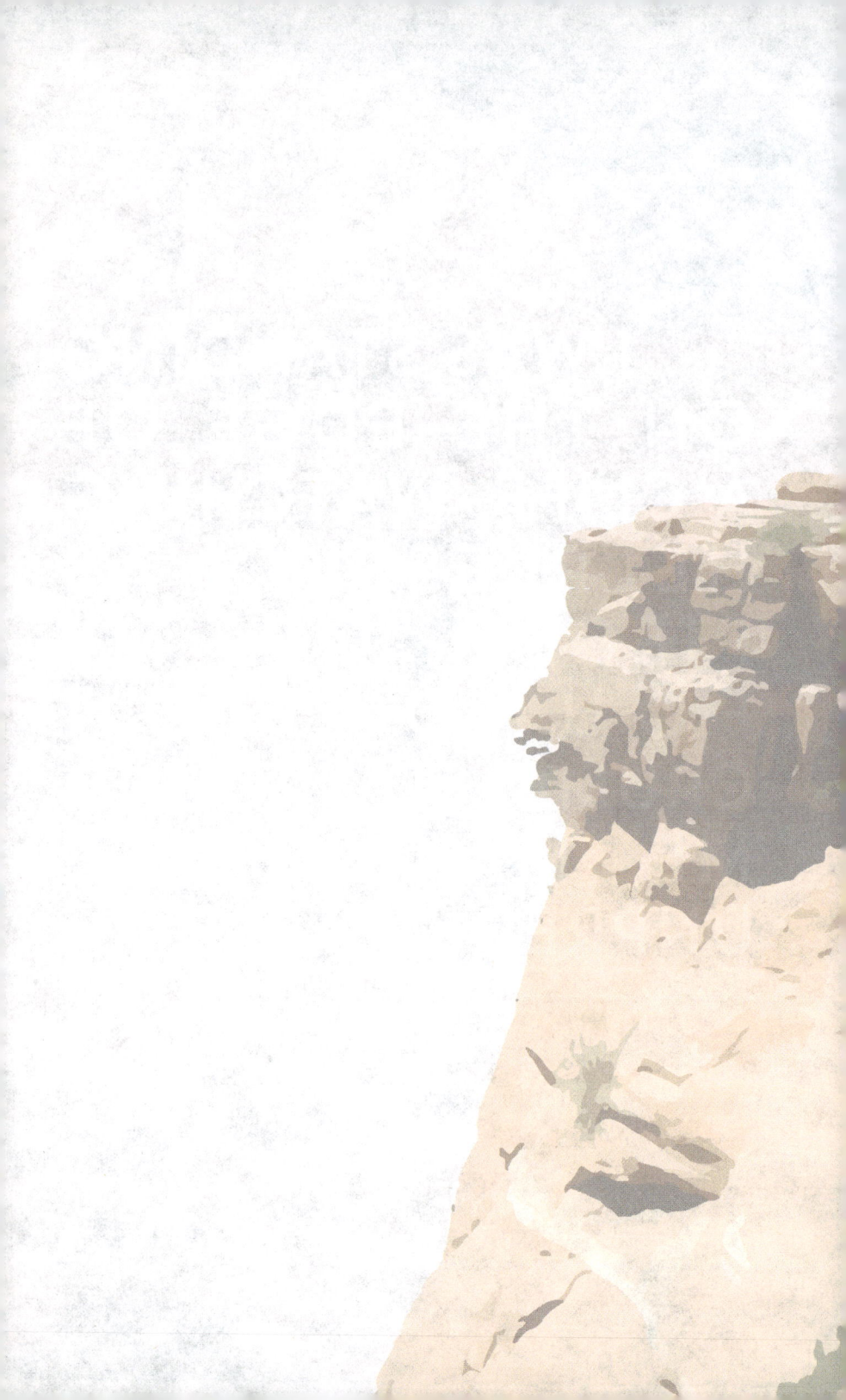

I KNOW A SECRET. GOD WHISPERED IT INTO THE AIR AND SENT IT DOWN TO ME. MY HEART HEARD IT.

In John 16:33, Jesus said,

> I have told you these things, so that in me you may have peace. In this world you will have trouble. But take heart! I have overcome the world.

I needed a Savior to bring me peace. I was standing on the edge of a cliff, watching helplessly as pieces of my foundation crumbled around me, making life unpredictable. My life seemed to be going 90 mph while my mind was in slow motion. By the time the two connected, I was lost in body, mind, and soul. These seemingly negative things happening in my life were not planned and left me feeling hopeless, scared, and at the mercy of the world.

I had built my life on prediction and planning. I set my mind on a goal and would achieve it through dedication and hard work. I had life figured out. Nothing could hold me back from being successful with everything I did because I was willing to put in the time to make it perfect. Isn't that what we learn in childhood? Study, share, love, believe, try harder. . . .

There's a quote that reads, "Everything I need to know, I learned in kindergarten." Here's what I learned in kindergarten.

"Dad" didn't walk me into kindergarten because he was in prison. From three to five years old, I didn't even have a memory of him aside from taking a picture by the painted mural of the Muskegon Correctional Facility and Cotton Facility in Jackson, both hours away from our house. My mom struggled to support my brother, sister, and me on a low income, so in school I had free lunch. The grocery store was for necessities and rarely for candy bars and gum in the checkout lane. Those items were considered special treats. My brother, sister, and I had to agree on one box of cereal at the store, while restaurants weren't something I was familiar with at that age. I wore my sister's clothes a lot of the time, something I can't say I minded because I looked up to her (even if she found me to be an annoying five year old). My siblings and I didn't have big, expensive toys, nor did we go on vacations.

Childhood also taught me that my sister was more popular, more beautiful, and more outgoing. I learned my brother was a better athlete. I came to the realization that my friends went to church, and we did not. They had married parents; I did not. They received multiple Christmas presents and would come to school showcasing them; I did not. I learned that when you let the dog out and nobody goes to get him, he ends up in the pound and eventually on a nice "farm" because it's too expensive to keep him.

I also learned the "normal" things in kindergarten—like when my big brother counts to three, something is going to happen. My older sister didn't want me wearing her clothes or hanging out with her. When Mom says clean, she means we have to lift things up and wipe under them. Don't leave dirty dishes by the bed for over a week. The dog will eat anything you leave out, including

Hershey's Kisses (that will cause a bigger mess later). Your brother will hide your toothbrush just to see if you brush your teeth in the morning. A new box of cereal doesn't last long in a house of three children. If you cry, Mom will come to your rescue and yell at whomever you blame.

When I was five years old, my father was released from prison and went into a halfway house. It was then I learned about interrupted sleep, fighting, and being scared. During the day my father was given permission to leave the halfway house to look for a job. Instead, he came into our house multiple times, threatening to take me from my mom and grabbing me from a deep sleep. I'd awaken to find them pulling at me, with my mom screaming at him to let me go. I learned that the happy family you see on old TV shows with the parents and siblings laughing and going on vacation together simply did not exist. It was imaginary—something that someone created.

Later in life, I can tell you that I looked back and learned so much more. I learned new designer clothes don't determine who you are. The brand of food doesn't matter as long as you're receiving nutrients. The car you drive doesn't matter as long as it can get you from point A to point B. All these things are nice, but we should feel blessed to have them. Tribulations can bring you closer together with family. People will walk out of your life, but it doesn't mean you have to follow them. Comfort isn't found in other people but in God Himself. You cannot change people; individuals must change themselves. Some things are completely out of your control, no matter how hard you try or how determined you might be. I've since learned that Christmas isn't about Santa

Claus unless your "Santa" is Jesus. Jesus is the one who brings us gifts—life. I can look back and know that religion, prayer, and knowledge of the Bible do make a difference. I learned not to make fun of people who are not as fortunate. Above all, I learned that God had a plan for me from the very beginning. He purposely chose my parents, knowing the choices they would make. He knew it would make me a more knowledgeable person who would desperately seek and find Him nineteen years later. He also knew that when I found Him, I'd never let Him go.

12 YEARS LATER

I had a dream. A man was walking toward me in a long robe. I ran, but every time I looked back at Him, He was there. Staring. Waiting. To this day, I can vividly remember His blue eyes. They were distinct, unique. Although light blue, they weren't a shade of color I'd ever seen before. They were beautiful! They seemed to combine a mixture of sky blue, the beauty and sparkle of the first snowfall, and the depth of the bluest, cleanest body of water I could imagine. They captured me . . . they scared me. Not in an "I'm going to be hurt" kind of way, but in an "I don't know him" way. He never posed a threat to me in the dream—He was just always behind me. It was snowing that night in the dream, so when I ran to my car, I found it was iced shut. I didn't dare look behind me because I knew He was there, and the thought terrified me. Like in the movies, my door opened at the last possible second . . . the second before the man could "get me." I was in an old car . . . old enough that you had to push the lock down by the window.

I sat scared in the passenger seat of the old car, staring up at the curly auburn-haired man with those unforgettable blue eyes. He was disappointed but completely relaxed and confident. He looked down at the lock, which was still up. He could open the door. My eyes followed His, and I immediately pushed the lock down, challenging His stare. His face dropped as He gazed at me. I felt regret build up inside me. I had made a mistake! He faded . . . or I faded . . . and I woke up crying with large sobs. I knew who He was. I was seventeen and had never met Him, but I recognized Him. I immediately knew what the dream meant as I sat crying in my bed. He came to warn me. I wrote down the entire dream, unable to get those blue eyes out of my mind. He never tried to hurt me; He was just pursuing me. He had no weapon, but I knew He was strong. He was everywhere! He was so close that He could have touched me at any time. Who was I to think I was smart enough to get away? Why would I want to get away from Him? The more I wrote down, the more I realized what the dream meant. It would taunt me for years. I had locked Jesus out of my life.

I'd spend the next year walking into churches alone, hoping to find something that felt "right." However, with no biblical background, I hardly understood anything the church was doing or saying. I quickly became discouraged.

I knew God. I knew parts of the Lord's Prayer, and I remember reciting a simple prayer before bedtime at my grandma's house. I can honestly say I had no idea what it meant, and nobody explained. Most of my family had grown up devoted Catholics but had found some reason to disconnect from the church, so when I grew up, there was no mention of it. I grew up with the idea that as long as you're a good person, you go to heaven. God is good, and He'd never send good people to hell.

I quit searching for a church, and the memory of the man in the dream faded. This wasn't God's plan, and life would make an intervention that I could not walk away from.

I started teaching special education at the age of twenty-one. After being voted teacher of the year among first-, second-, and third-year teachers in the county, I proceeded to complete my master's degree in administration three years later. Academic work in college came easy to my overactive mind. I dove deeper into the education field, signing up to be on state committees regarding statewide testing and even being in charge of a statewide professional development conference in the special education field by the age of twenty-five. Although successful, none of this made me happy. I wasn't the little girl who dreamed of being a teacher. It wasn't even my second choice. I was the girl who dreamed of being the female version of Stephen King or a veterinarian. When I learned that creativity would allow me to be anywhere, anytime, I fell deep into the world of writing. I wasn't a straight-A student, so my dreams of being a vet seemed like a goal I'd never achieve. On the other hand, writing came easily. Beginning at age eight, I wasn't found running around the park with friends but rather sitting at a picnic table writing chapter books about murder and tragedy.

With the discouragement that writing wouldn't give me a secure future, I went with option three—teaching sign language. However, the lack of job opportunity led me to become a teacher for those with cognitive impairments.

I knew I wasn't happy teaching, but I had no idea what to do with that knowledge. I was doing a job that I was good at . . . I enjoyed the kids . . . I made good money . . . I had a good retirement. What was wrong with me? I didn't feel complete.

I was intrigued with medicine, so I decided to stay in teaching and work part-time as an EMT. A year later, I was working for an ambulance company. It didn't help. God was telling me my life was missing something. He was showing me through feelings, experience, and people.

There's a popular story in the Bible about Jonah. If you know even a small amount about the Bible, you can probably recall that a sea creature we believe would be equivalent to a whale swallowed Jonah. That's not what I'm hoping you remember about Jonah. Jonah was told by God to go to Nineveh on a difficult mission. He ran in the other direction to Tarshish, which is why the sea creature swallowed him.

I was Jonah. God had tried time and time again to direct me in the path He had chosen for me, but time and time again I refused to listen, doing what I thought was easiest and best for me at that time. I was stubborn and attempted to take every other path aside from the one He wanted me to take.

I became unhappy with life with no reason to be. I was a successful teacher who had graduated with honors with a master's degree and EMT license. I married my first serious boyfriend after dating five years, and together we bought a beautiful, expensive home. Together we made enough money to enjoy life without the worry of living paycheck to paycheck.

Aside from a steady relationship, I had also traveled to all fifty states and nine countries. I'd seen Big Ben and the Eye, Billy Joel play a free concert in front of the Coliseum, the winding rivers of Venice, the paintings in Florence, *The Last Supper* painting in Milan, beautiful beaches in the Caribbean, and flamenco dancing in Spain. I had gone cliff diving in Mexico and had eaten lunch gazing at the mountains in Switzerland. I'd traveled from the glamor of California to the Bad Lands of South Dakota to the sunny beaches of South Carolina. I'd seen the glaciers of Alaska, ridden high above Florida in a hot-air balloon, and swum with the sharks in Hawaii. I was coaching sports for Special Olympics, engaged in numerous volunteer projects throughout the year, and had finally found a church and been baptized. I was healthy, active, and winning first place in martial arts tournaments throughout the state. My life was blessed, and it seemed that everything I touched turned to success. It seemed that life was perfect.

Four years after getting married, I was filing for divorce from the man I'd been with for nine years. We were disconnected, and I knew neither one of us had the strength or faith needed to make it a successful marriage. I was no longer a priority to him, and he no longer had my heart. I was angry, hurt, and disappointed at myself, him, and God. How did we get along so well in the beginning but have such very different ideas of life in the end?

My string of unfortunate events didn't end there. I was going to specialists and surgeons for a back injury caused from martial arts, vomiting up meals involuntarily from what turned out to be a pre-cancerous ulcer in my esophagus, attempting to pay off mounds of student loans, and losing faith that there was anyone decent left in administration of the educational field. Work became more of a burden than a love of mine. It was never the kids but rather that I disagreed so much with administration. I felt a lack of control to change a situation I had to deal with daily. It seemed as if every area of my life were falling apart. I felt as if I were on the edge of a high mountain with the ground crumbling beneath me.

Looking back, there are few people I'd say I loved aside from my ex-husband. There are men I deeply cared for and sincerely hope are doing well, but there have only been one or two that I could see a future with. "He" was one of them. From the moment I saw his blue eyes, I knew I'd never be the same. It was like a magnetic pull, the moment where the world stops spinning and you focus on that one person and only that person. I saw a future . . . I felt a feeling. Our conversations were easy, enjoyable, and always left me feeling like they had just begun. Days turned into months and then years, and while things progressed, in the end they remained the same. He simply was not willing to act on how he said he felt. I felt loss again and was hurt and confused how something that felt so right could be wrong.

For years I asked myself, "What happened?" What happened to contentment? What happened to happiness? Looking back, I'm confident of the answer. Life happened. God happened. He had something much better planned for me, but it was in His timing . . . His perfect timing.

I've been through the struggle. I've felt hurt, sadness, disappointment, and fear. I know how it feels to not have Plan A, Plan B, or Plan C work out. I've questioned God. I've been mad at Him, speaking to Him through clenched teeth. I've looked at situations and thought, "Well, God, You didn't show up for this person, did You?" I've looked at my own situations and thought sarcastically, "Why don't You just throw something else on me too?" I've questioned the work of God many, many times!

While I debated whether or not to share such personal information, I felt it necessary to show that I've been there. To write well, you have to write what you know. I know difficulty. I know struggle. I know fear. I know anger. I know abandonment. I know confusion. I know disruption in the mind and heart. I know love that doesn't last. I know that feeling when you just don't have the answer you're looking for. Helpless. Hopeless. Faithless. I *know*. While our situations are not the same, the solution is the same.

I've always wanted to be a writer, but I never had a story I wanted to share. I had numerous questions in life that I not only *wanted* answered; I *needed* them to be answered. To find those answers, I needed to do something I hadn't done before . . . to be alone physically and mentally. I desired to run, to get away from my life and all the struggles within it. I needed to search for my missing soul. I was lost and knew I needed to find myself before I ended up in a place I didn't want to be: a dark, lonely, and endless path.

I'd always felt a connection to Sedona, Arizona. From the moment I saw the red rocks and lush green forest, I fell in love. The green and red mixture mesmerized me from the start. Now at a point in my life when everything seemed to be crumbling, I didn't give it much thought before paying for one roundtrip ticket to the beautiful red rock country. Intuition told me I'd find peace there. I prayed to God that night and asked Him to come with me—just us—for the next four days with no distractions. I wanted to get to know Him better, although *better* isn't really a good description since I didn't know Him at all. I didn't grow up attending church, and I wasn't even baptized until I was 24. After my rebirth, my definition of being religious meant attending church on Sundays—if I woke up on time. Now life was continuously disappointing, and I desperately needed strength, courage, and wisdom. I was exhausted from negative emotions, so I turned over all the battles in my mind to Him and asked for His help with this prayer:

Dear God,

I pray for complete serenity, peace, and calmness for the entire body, mind, heart, and soul. I imagine that they do exist because to doubt their existence is to doubt the power within You. Where does peace exist? A mountain? The forest? A vortex? In death? In heaven? In ourselves? Can it be found with noise, obligations, and in the presence of negative people at work? I pray for a different life!

I want a life where I give unconditionally and feel control/happiness/calmness in one breath. I pray for You to change me, guide me, and help me find my destination so that you can work through me. I desire to be in the right place at the right time, all the time. I want to change the world with You by my side.

I believe all things are possible through You. All life's questions can be answered, but I need to know how to listen. Right now I do not hear you. I know You, but I have not learned how to communicate with You. Guide me. Show me. Be with me always.

I feel sad. I feel confused. I feel alone. I feel pressured. I feel like there's a constant battle in my head. I feel like my heart and brain are not linked. I feel tired. I feel guilty. I feel abandoned.

God, I also believe the world is beautiful. I feel empathy for people. I appreciate the small things You put in front of me. I am hopeful that bad people can be good. I am compassionate to those who are less fortunate. I believe in true love and a fairy-tale ending. I think all things in life happen for a reason. I think life is our greatest gift.

I am going to take a trip with You. Just us. I want to get to know You better; I need to know myself better. I have questions that only You know the answers to that deal with location, love, and career. I am looking forward to the next four days with You. No phone, no computer, no family or friends . . . just the two of us.

I know this vacation will bring us closer together, and I'm excited to have our relationship go to a deeper level. You are the most important person in my life, and there's no other person I'd rather be with than You. Thank You for having faith in me. I know you are the answer to every question. All I ask is that You help me learn to listen with my heart and shut off my mind.

I am ready to start life . . . the right way, Your way.

Amen.

Somehow I knew that in only four days, I'd have the "secret"... the answer . . . the truth to all the answers I was seeking. This is *my* story written for *you*.

> And the God of all grace, who called you to his eternal glory in Christ, after you have suffered a little while, will himself restore you and make you strong, firm and steadfast. To him be the power forever and ever. Amen.
>
> ~ 1 Peter 5:10–11

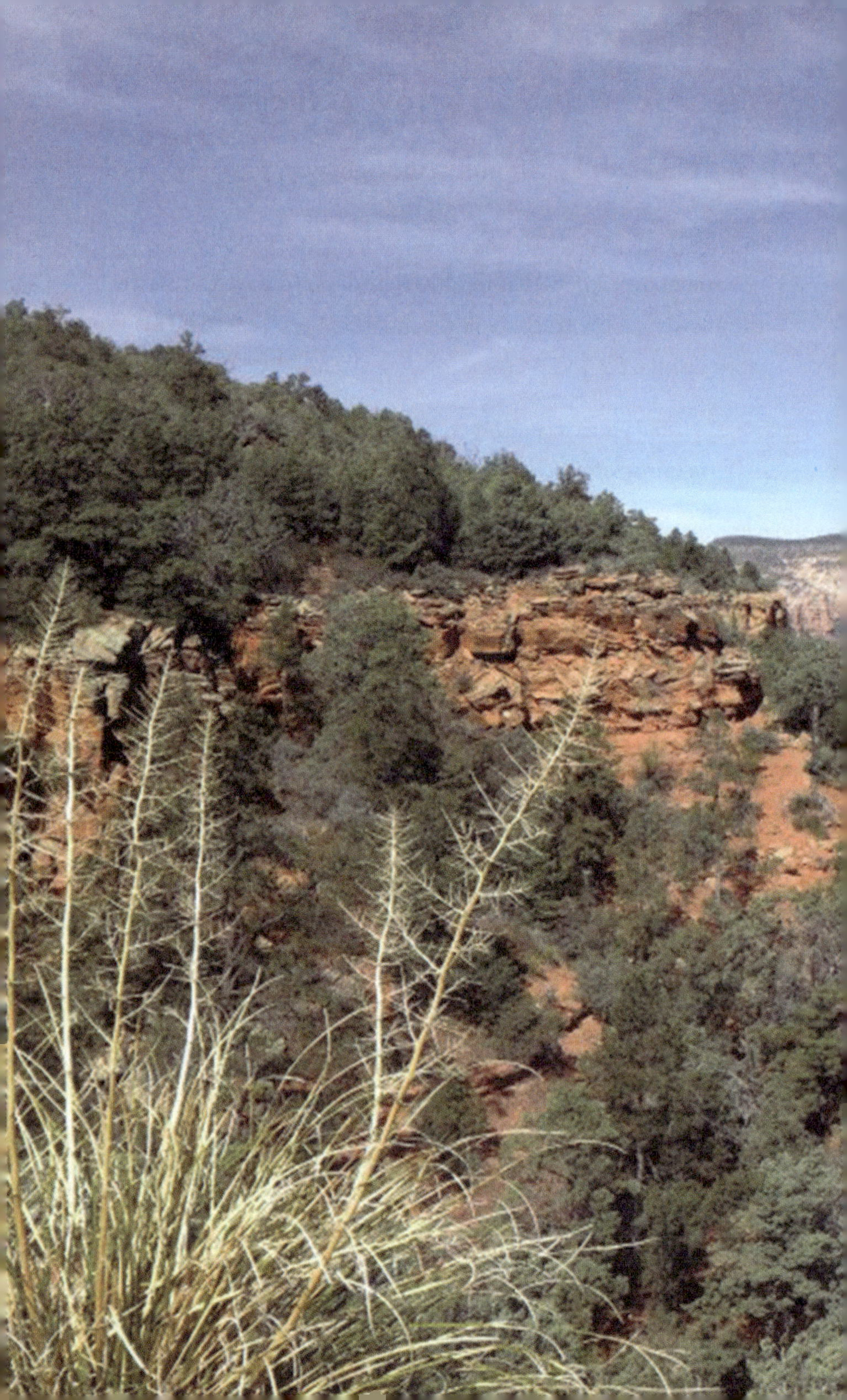

". . . GOD, HELP ME!" I PLEADED. "WHERE ARE MY ANSWERS? I'M LOST, AND I FEEL ALONE . . ."

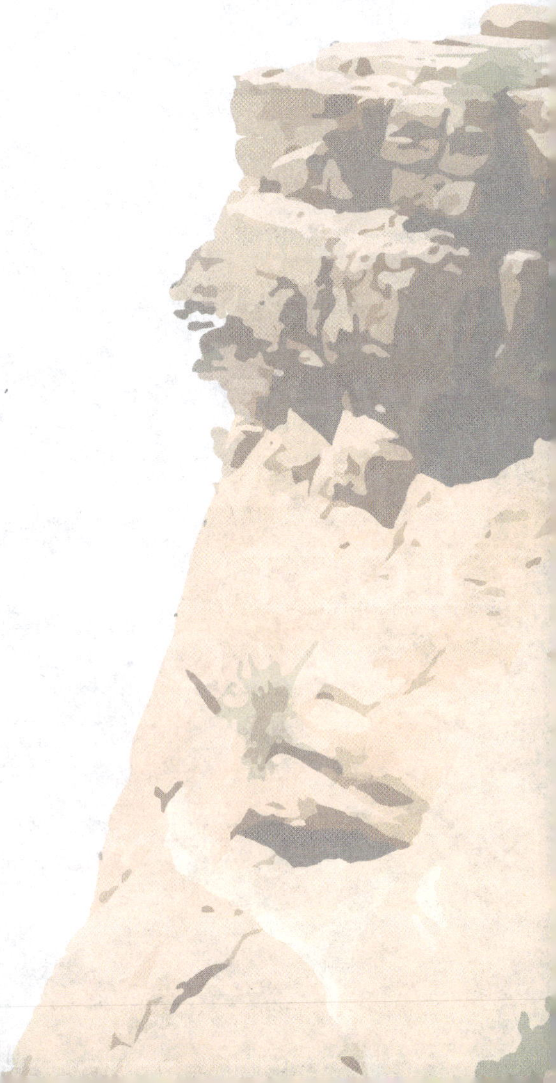

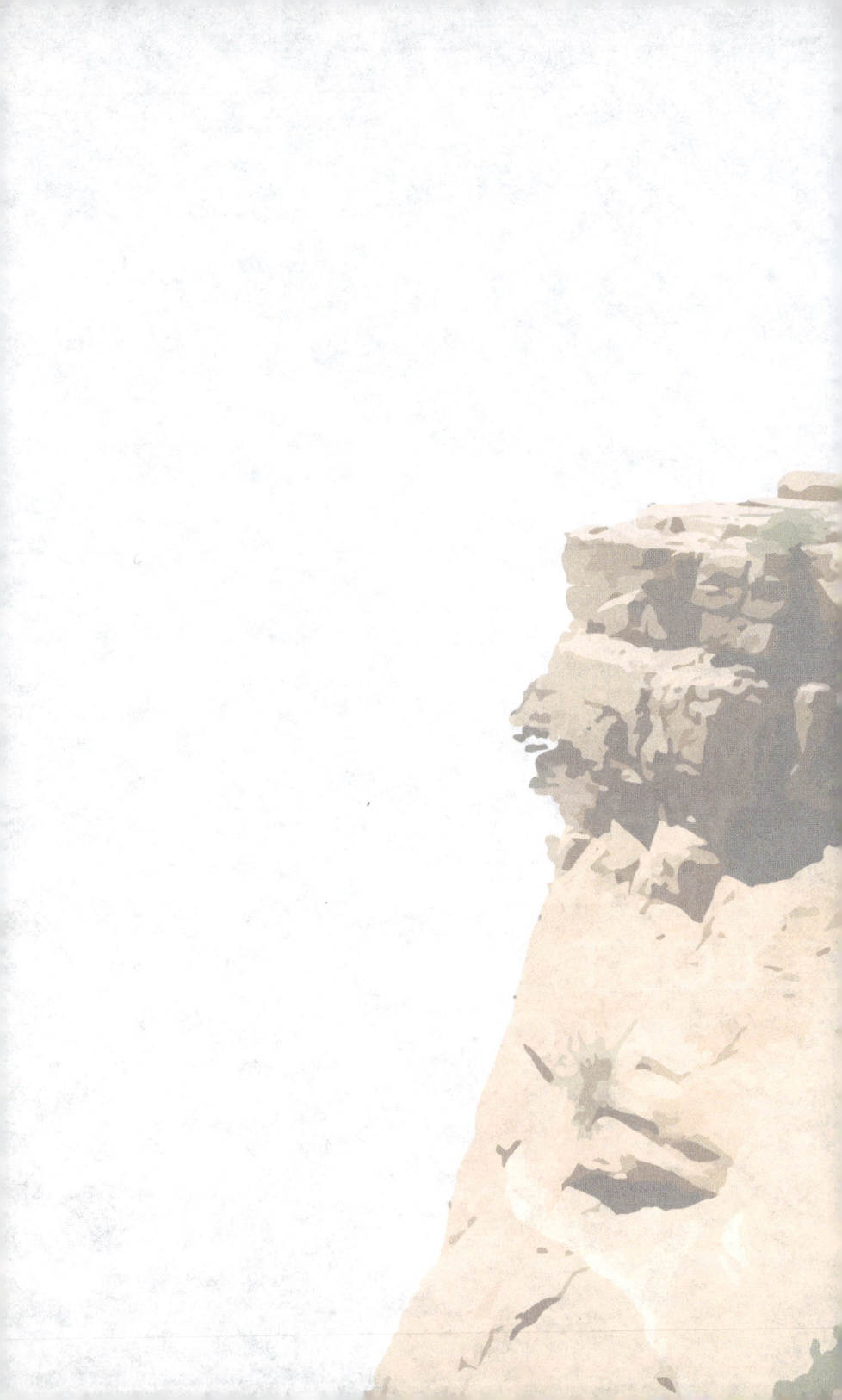

CHAPTER 1

EVERYTHING IS MEANINGLESS

For I am the Lord your God who takes hold of your right hand and says to you, Do not fear; I will help you.

~ Isaiah 41:13

I do not know the answers, but I know the questions.

I do not know the conditions of your trail, but I know the gear you should wear.

I do not know your destination, but I can give you a map.

I am not a therapist, but I can offer guidance.

I am not a nun, but I can offer comfort.

I am not a guru, but I can offer peace.

Each life on earth is different, and the path we take will never be exactly the same as any other. As humans we tend to seek answers from each other. The bad news is there's not a single person on earth who has all the answers you seek. The good news is that there are answers to every situation you can ever think to create. However, the only one who can provide you the comfort, peace, and love you ask for is God, and He's already doing it! God made you perfect. When you were born, you were packaged with everything you'd need for your journey in life; however, instead of believing that we are born with this innate ability to just "know" all our solutions, many people spend some, most, or all of their lives asking, searching, and reading to find them. We want solutions, and most people want them to be easy.

Believing the answer is already within us means we have to know ourselves and put in the effort to figure out the solution. Our brains don't just outwardly say, "Here's the solution!" That would make life . . . well . . . boring! We need to experience tears, death of loved ones, and failure by humans to realize how great our God truly is.

If everything in your life was good and went exactly the way *you* wanted it to go, then where would you be? Would you be a famous rock star in a band? Would you be the greatest doctor in the world? Would you be a stay-at-home father? If God let everything go according to *your* plan, would you be happy with your life? Until we follow our Creator's plan, I'm convinced we will always live in a life where everything is never enough. When we follow our own plan and ignore God's, we consciously or subconsciously keep searching for something to fill the void felt. We keep buying, reaching, doing, and are never content. Living life to our own desires creates an obscure view of what happiness really is. We are wrong to believe happiness is found in items, people, awards, jobs, or getting our way.

> "Meaningless! Meaningless!" says the Teacher. "Utterly meaningless! Everything is meaningless." What do people gain from all their labors at which they toil under the sun? Generations come and generations go, but the earth remains forever. The sun rises and the sun sets, and hurries back to where it rises. The wind blows to the south and turns to the north; round and round it goes, ever returning on its course. All streams flow into the sea, yet the sea is never full. To the place the streams come from, there they return again. All things are wearisome, more than one can say. The eye never has enough of seeing, nor the ear its fill of hearing. What has been will be again, what has been done will be done again; there is nothing new under the sun. Is there anything of which one can say, "Look! This is something new"? It was here already, long ago; it was here before our time.
>
> ~ Ecclesiastes 1:2–10

Without Jesus, our lives will eventually turn to dust, which makes everything done on earth meaningless. There's nothing we are able to do on earth if it were not for the grace of God. It exists only because He created it. He makes the sun rise and set each day and calls to the wind to blow to the north or south. Without Him, none of it would exist and without Him, none of it matters. A person who accomplishes great things on earth will, too, turn to dust and one day be forgotten if he doesn't believe in Jesus.

God is waiting for a relationship with you. That doesn't mean going to church or praying at night (yes, these things are included and important), but it means having a daily conversation with Him, living a life He would be proud of, and doing as the Bible instructs. Having a relationship with God is so much more than attending service on Sunday morning. It's more than praying before meals or praying when you need help. Having a relationship with God is available right now. Our Creator is always next to you and waiting for you to talk to Him.

Remove yourself as a priority, realize that all your problems in life are only important on the earth (meaningless dust), and this life is only the beginning of a much more beautiful, incredible journey. God has given us a gift through His Son, Jesus. He has given you the chance to have eternal life, but you must accept the gift. Your life is not going to start until you begin moving, and if you stay in one place, *life* will pass you by. You get one chance to do it right. Do it according to God's standards, not your own. If you do it right, you only need one chance.

As long as you keep yourself as a priority, you will continue to be living in a world mixed with confusion, anger, disappointment, sadness, and guilt. You will keep changing jobs, losing friends, and struggling day to day. The person who believes he can find happiness without God will wake up one morning and acknowledge that "feeling"—the emptiness and disconnect from the world—and wonder what would really make him happy. Our focus need not be on ourselves but on our Savior. Placing God as priority doesn't mean that you won't ask yourself life's hardest questions: How do I get out of debt? Why do I feel so tired all the time? Why did I get cancer? Why doesn't she love me? Why don't my friends call? Why can't I have children? Why do my children act like this? Why did I lose an arm? Why am I overweight? Why can't I find a job I enjoy? Why do good things happen to bad people? Why do bad things happen to good people? Why . . . Why . . . Why?

How well has that "why" question served you in the past? You're not wrong for asking the question, but are you getting very far by asking your neighbor, mate, family members, or friends that question? Obviously not because you're reading . . . searching . . . curious . . . hoping someone has an answer to that question you've been asking yourself. There *is* an answer, and you already have it.

> I can provide a map, but it's your responsibility to follow it.

> I can tell you the equipment needed for your trip, but you must use it.

> I can provide you words of knowledge, but you must listen to them.

Before you ever took your first breath, God loved you. He gave you to your parents with a beautifully designed plan. He gave you away, but He never gave you up. He's supporting you every day. His shoulder carries your racing fears, His finger smooths away your tears, and His words encourage you every second. He's promised to never leave you or forsake you. God wants you to be confident and walk down the path He's designed for you. However, if we choose to ignore the supports God gives us, if we give in to feelings of negativity, then it's much more difficult to reach true happiness. God will always support and comfort you. God will give you things you have not worked for nor deserved; however, you must accept his gifts and let Him guide you.

God may have planned for you to become a traveling missionary. He may have equipped you with great communication skills, a desire to teach and help, and a love for traveling. But if you let fear of disease, terrorist attacks, flight troubles, crowded airports, new languages, and not "knowing enough" stop you from participating in the mission trip that just "unexpectedly" came up, you will never follow God's plan. God will keep leading you back to where He originally wanted you to be, but the sad truth is that not everyone will follow His lead.

You must walk confidently, and you have every reason to do so. Philippians 4:13 reads, "I can do all this through him who gives me strength." Why shouldn't we be confident in life if Christ gives us strength? It doesn't mean you won't fall. Babies learn to walk, but they fall a lot. Facing obstacles and overcoming them teaches us much more than to have something handed freely to us. Perhaps the object is not to overcome the obstacle at all but just to learn from it. Talk about difficult to understand. We see it as a failure if we can't accomplish something we put our minds to. Hard work should result in success. It does. The problem is how we define success.

God's way isn't always our way. God's timing isn't always our timing. It's hard to realize that life is completely out of our control because we were never intended to be in control of it. That's why God should be the priority in our life and serve as a constant reminder that we are living for Him and not ourselves.

You want an answer of some kind. Maybe you want to grow in faith, have resolution to a struggle, or you simply just found the title entertaining. Picking up this book is purposeful, and so is God's plan for you!

Peace does exist in a world of disappointment and turmoil. There is a moment in your life that will come when you realize that every event up to that point was meaningful and purposeful. If you want to reach that picture-perfect moment, you can. You just have to walk there. *Walk.*

Life is unpredictable even when there is planning. Sometimes our path gets slippery, narrow, steep, and dark. Maybe those things include death, an unexpected diagnosis, wrongful accusations, abandonment, neglect, guilt, or financial distress. If you live long enough, you will most likely suffer from all of these. Nobody has a path in life that is free from despair, suffering, or detours. The only people who ever saw a path so easy were Adam and Eve before sin entered the world.

As an adult, you can control your decisions, but life will most definitely take you to places you never expected to be, both good and bad. Life seems to be going great, but in one split second, something happens, and you are thrown into a world of chaos. You are most definitely in control of your decisions—but never believe you are in control of life. It will prove you wrong time and time again. By making good choices in life, your path has the potential to take you to places beyond your imagination. God wants great things for you! When we continuously make bad decisions (those that go against the Bible), we end up lost and fail to move forward. Lost is lost. Sin is sin.

There's plenty of sin in the world, and we all are guilty of committing it. While sin appears in various forms in people, it all amounts to the same thing in God's eyes: disappointment. We don't deserve heaven because we are all sinners. Every person in the Bible was a sinner except Jesus. Some committed adultery, some worshipped idols, others refused to help their neighbor, many ran from God's word and refused to listen to His instructions, many lost faith in God when things didn't go their way, and some simply didn't believe. The Old Testament of the Bible will bring you through a number of dramatic events. Entire cities were destroyed because of sin, armies were overtaken, people were captured, and executions took place, and it was all a result of sin.

God didn't say, "Adultery is less of an offense than idol worship." He didn't say, "Refusing to help those in need is not nearly as bad as refusing to listen to My instructions." No. You can read the Bible again and again, but you won't find sins listed on tiered levels. Are you wondering why? Sin is sin, just as an apple is an apple. You can call an apple a fruit or make it into applesauce. You can fry apples, cook them, boil them, chop them, slice them, dip them in caramel and cover them, or let them grow on a tree until they rot. The origin of the caramel apple, applesauce, and fried apple was an apple. The origin of adultery, idol worship, taking God's name in vain, theft, murder, jealousy, dishonoring your mother and father, not keeping the Sabbath, lying, etc. was and always will be sin. It's written. We call them the Ten Commandments, but number one is no more important than ten. We were born sinners. We will always be sinners. We will die sinners. We don't deserve heaven because we are not perfect in thought, word, and deed. Our sins deserve maximum punishment because we are here for God, and our sin means we have gone against Him. God hears our thoughts, and it would be another sin to say we always have good thoughts. If we didn't have the New Testament, there would be no hope.

Consider yourself light years ahead when you come to the realization that you don't deserve heaven or God's forgiveness of your sins. That is how great our God is! He does forgive our sins, and He has opened up the gates of heaven for us. He did all this through His one and only Son. God gave us more than hope; He gave us salvation: Jesus Christ.

DAY 1 OF VACATION 2012: SEDONA, ARIZONA

With my Red Rock parking permit safely tucked away in my hiking bag, I stepped out of the chamber of commerce in downtown Sedona. I was greeted by heavy rain that instantly drenched my hiking pants and loose-fitted T-shirt. People rushed under the shelter of the building, but I embraced the gift from God by opening my arms and letting the rain soak every inch of my body as I slowly walked to my car. I had hiking plans, and rain was not going to stop me from venturing to the first trail: Airport Loop.

Since it was only 1:00 PM, I decided to check into the Sky Ranch Lodge first. I received a free upgrade to a room with a fireplace and private balcony upon my check-in. I couldn't help but believe a positive attitude with the rain and the excitement of being in Sedona with God had something to do with my good fortune.

I didn't waste any time changing clothes and venturing to my first trail, which was only a half-mile from the lodge. I hadn't done a lot of research on vortexes, but I knew a vortex existed at the Airport Trail. Without a strong religious background, I was intrigued by what a vortex symbolized. They are said to facilitate prayer. At a weak, hopeless point in my life, I became driven to find God through one.

My plan was to spend the day reading the Bible and writing whatever came to my mind. This was my chosen form of meditation—my way of finding answers to life's most difficult questions. I'd never read the Bible before. In fact, I saw it as a book of names and locations that were hard to pronounce, along with a bunch of stories that didn't seem to have any impact on my life now. I knew I'd be reading about God, but to my limited knowledge, none of these "characters" in the Bible knew God, so therefore I assumed the book was composed of a bunch of heresy. Nevertheless, I had brought it and was determined to read it in the hope that I'd find some kind of comfort to ease my guilt, suffering, and disappointment with life.

When I arrived at the trail marker, I paused. To the left of me, there were people climbing on large red rocks; their conversations and laughter echoed off the rocks. To the right of me was the start of Airport Loop, a trail that would lead me to walk around the edge of the mountain. No sign of a vortex.

I proceeded down the Airport Loop Trail and hesitated about 500 feet along the edge of the mountain. The rain had made the trail slick, and loose gravel rolled away from my feet. I looked at the area I was about to step in and knew that if I slipped, I would fall hundreds of feet off the edge. I tried to peer around the rocks to get a view of the path past this particular place. "Go back." Inside my head, a silent voice told me not to proceed. I let out a sigh; was it intuition or fear? What's the difference between the two? I turned back around and went to the trailhead to assure myself that I was actually on a trail. During my many hiking trips, I'd certainly gone off trail a time or two. Back at the trailhead, my attention was drawn back to the red rocks on the left. There was no mistake. There was only one direction for the trail. I glanced back at the people climbing on the red rocks and taking pictures of Sedona's undeniable beauty. I just wanted to sit and read. I'd been in the airplane and car most of the day, and I was finally ready to think about my life and cry if I needed to. Every part of me was anxious for the opportunity to sit in silence and reflect on the events in my life.

"Find the vortex and you can sit," I said softly to myself. I forced myself to go over the loose gravel and continue on the trail, excited to get to the end of it. Over a mile later, I could feel myself become tense. I was alone. I imagined a wild animal coming down from a cliff or a snake wiggling from beneath a rock. I had no protection, and I hadn't passed another hiker.

At the moment I was debating whether or not to turn around, a runner came from the opposite direction. He nodded as he hurried past me, retracing my steps. "I guess I'm not completely alone," I said, relaxing and pausing to take a few pictures.

With each step I took, I became more excited about the vortex. I silently wondered how it was going to affect me and how long it would take to find the answers to my questions. Each corner I turned, I was greeted with disappointment. I wasn't near any vortex but instead a narrow trail that seemed to have endless trees and dirt. My greatest disappointment came when the trail ended before the end. The dirt path I had been following for the last mile and a half was now a muddy creek with small stones and bushes. Since I had been hiking in Arizona before, I knew that some trails broke up to go over creeks or rocks. I looked ahead as far as I could but saw no trace of a trail. I crossed the small creek, slipping on the mud from all the rain and proceeded to climb up the slight incline, maneuvering around the tree branches and bushes. I walked a few feet and stopped. No path. I jumped over the creek again; nothing. Panic took over my mind, and I found myself frantically searching for the path I'd just come on. How many times did I cross the creek? It's the first day, and I'm lost!

"Focus!" I closed my eyes and started to talk out loud, reminding myself to be calm. "Find your bearings. You're fine!"

I climbed to the top of a small hill and immediately saw the path. Irritated with myself, I climbed down and proceeded back on the trail the same way I'd come. This trail was not leading me to any vortex! I could feel tears well up in my eyes as I retraced my steps. I wasn't crying from the trail but because of life. Couldn't anything be in my favor . . . even something as simple as a trail? I just wanted answers! Where were my answers? Not getting any kind of answer, I started to run on the narrow trail. OUCH! I was immediately stopped when cactus needles entered my legs. I looked down at my knee. It had a small trickle of blood and dozens of small cactus splinters. I rolled my eyes, ignored them, and started to run again; I just wanted to be done and off this trail! I wanted to go back to the lodge, fill up a hot bath, and cry. Life was not on my side, and it hadn't been for a long time. OUCH! More cacti pricked my knees and now my left hand. Annoyed, I stopped to sit down. I knew I should have pulled out my tweezers from my hiking bag to remove the needles appropriately, but I didn't care. I was angry, impatient, and frustrated. I had just hiked 1.5 miles after sitting on an airplane and in a car all day, and this wasn't even a trail with a vortex!

"What am I doing here?" I asked out loud as I pulled out the cactus splinters. Those in my leg came out easily, but to this day, I still have broken-off pieces in my left finger. I don't even try to remove them, as they are a constant reminder of what I learned.

I unsnapped my hiking bag and continued to sit, gazing at the surrounding beautiful red rock mountains. What was happening? Why was I so anxious? "God, help me!" I pleaded. "Where are my answers? I'm lost, and I feel alone."

I sat long enough to regain my lost energy. Just as I stood up, the familiar runner was coming toward me again. He coasted from a run to a walk as he neared me.

"Hi," I said, moving over on the trail. "Hey, this is a trail that loops, right? Why did it dead end?"

He grinned. "Oh, you have to climb up the creek a little."

I nodded as I watched him pass me by. I hadn't trusted there would be a trail, and I retreated without much thought. Now here I was retracing every step I'd just taken over the last hour. Ugh! The answer hit me like a punch in the face. Fear. I had let fear control my actions again. This was a vacation with God and time to focus on myself, yet I was doing the same things I could be found doing at home. Wait. God! God! I let out a deep breath and put my hands together in prayer.

"God, I'm sorry. Here I am on vacation with You, and I've ignored You since I started hiking. I want to be here with You, I want You in my life, and I want to listen to what You have to say. I'm ready now."

I didn't wait for an answer because I just felt the need to confess. I felt every negative emotion wash away from me and be replaced with happiness and excitement. I paused numerous times to take in the scenery and to breathe in the fresh air.

As I exited the trail and looked over to the red rock that had caught my attention before I started the hike, I couldn't help but laugh out loud. Twisted trees lined the red rocks. I had read that they are a sign of energy from a vortex. "Well, I guess that was intuition," I silently told myself as I remembered debating where to go. I hurried over to the red rocks and climbed to the top. Flat! No trees! No reason to think I was in a vortex! I looked over at the trees that were growing out of the red rocks, unreachable.

Admitting defeat, I took my Bible out of my bag and started to read. Tears overcame me, and I found myself letting go of every question I'd had about life, health, love, family, career, and happiness. I acknowledged that despite success and so many great things happening in my life, I was sad. I began to pray again until I heard loud voices behind me. The language was one I did not understand, and I found myself annoyed with them. Didn't they know this was a place to be quiet? I stood up, wiped my tears, and shot them a disapproving glance.

I had finished a book on the plane and had written a little, but I was still feeling defeated. I couldn't write on a trail where I was alone; I couldn't write with these people; what had I come to Sedona for? I stepped down on the trail and immediately noticed a young girl sitting peacefully under a twisted tree on the other side of the rocks. I was intrigued and sat down to watch, or rather study, her. How was she able to shut the world out? After a few hours she stood up and left. I immediately took her place, and within seconds I could feel peace overtake my body. I had found a vortex!

I read the entire Book of John and wrote numerous pages in my journal. I was writing! I was reading! I was praying with intent! *This* is exactly where I was supposed to be. I spent more than five hours sitting in that place, unsure if I would ever get up. God and I were connecting for the first time, and I didn't want to let Him go—I wanted to stay in the moment forever. I wondered if I should return to this exact place every day and throw away my agenda.

God and I bonded that night. I felt like He wrapped His arms around me, let me cry, and repeatedly told me that He'd always be there. Day one of my journey taught me that the world will give you trouble, just as Jesus promised, but nothing is too big for Him. He let me know it's okay to cry. It's okay to be sad. It's okay to question the direction my life is taking. It's okay to live life and feel everything that life has to offer, including what we perceive as negative. Those moments of sadness make us stronger. Those moments of sadness help us appreciate the wonderful things God has put in front of us. Those moments of sadness can help bring us closer to our true Father, the one who will never leave you, just as He promised in Hebrews 13:5:

> Keep your lives free from the love of money and be content with what you have, because God has said, "Never will I leave you; never will I forsake you."

The only thing to remember . . .

> For God so loved the world that he gave his one and only Son, that whoever believes in him shall not perish but have eternal life.
>
> ~ John 3:16

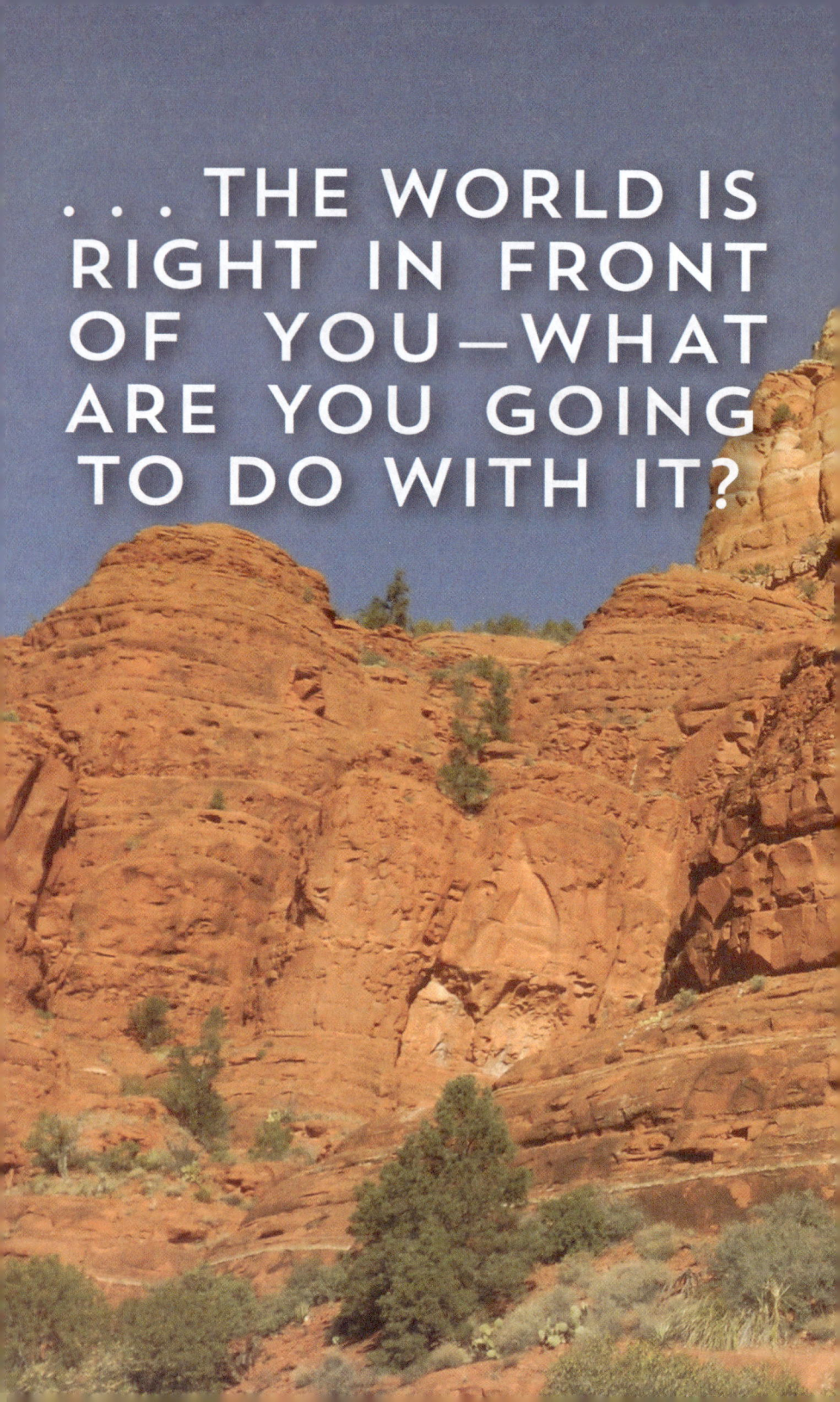

. . . THE WORLD IS RIGHT IN FRONT OF YOU—WHAT ARE YOU GOING TO DO WITH IT?

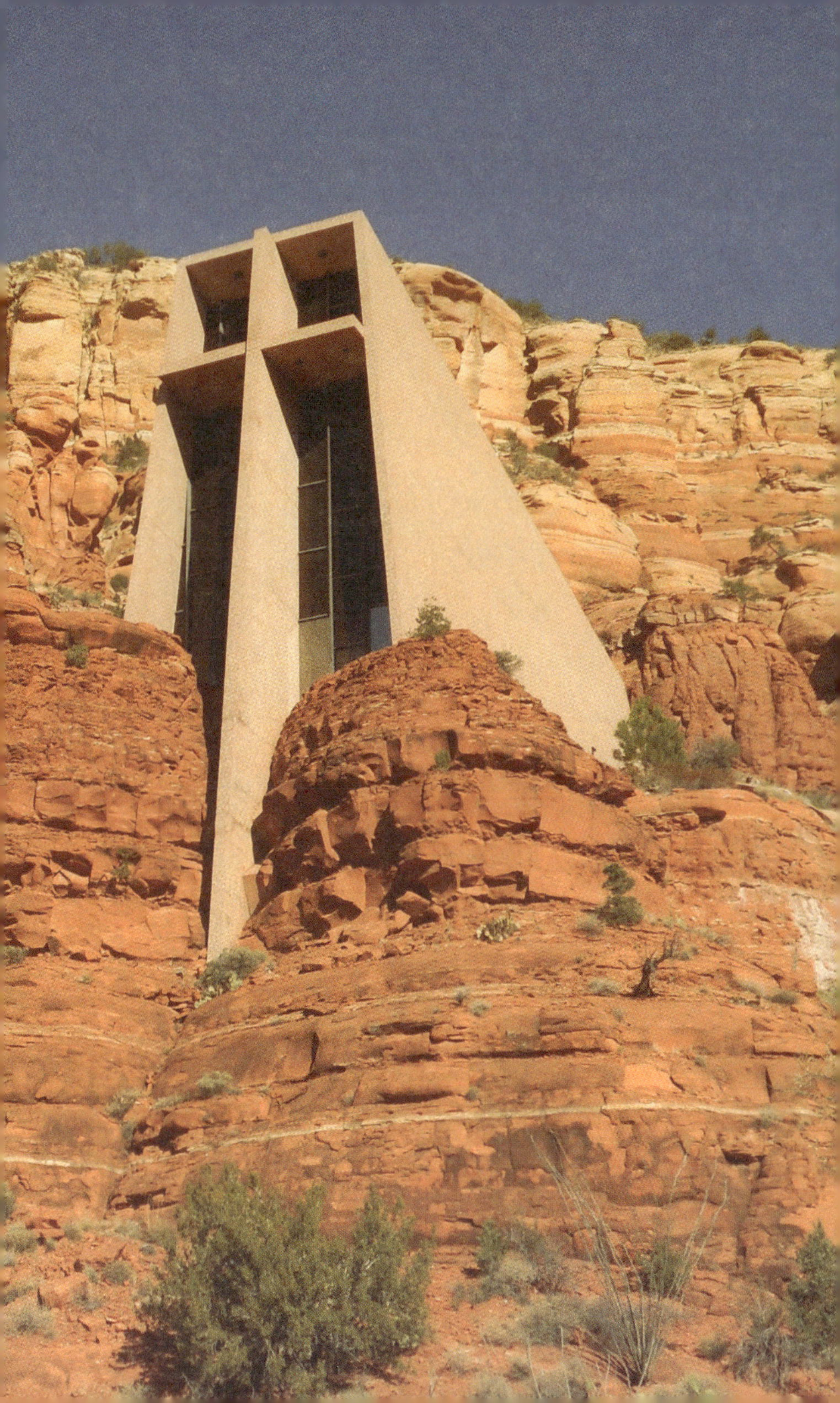

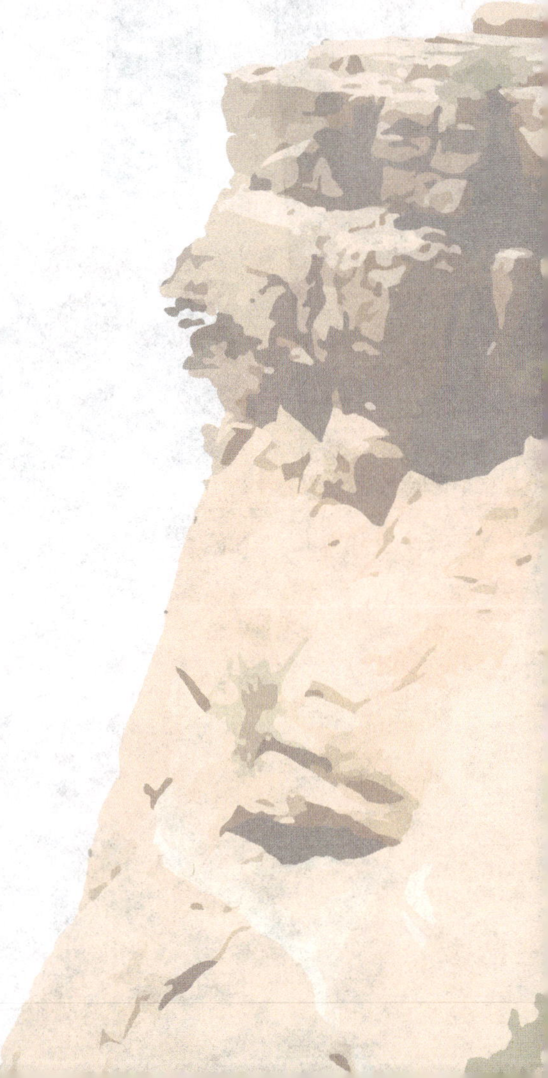

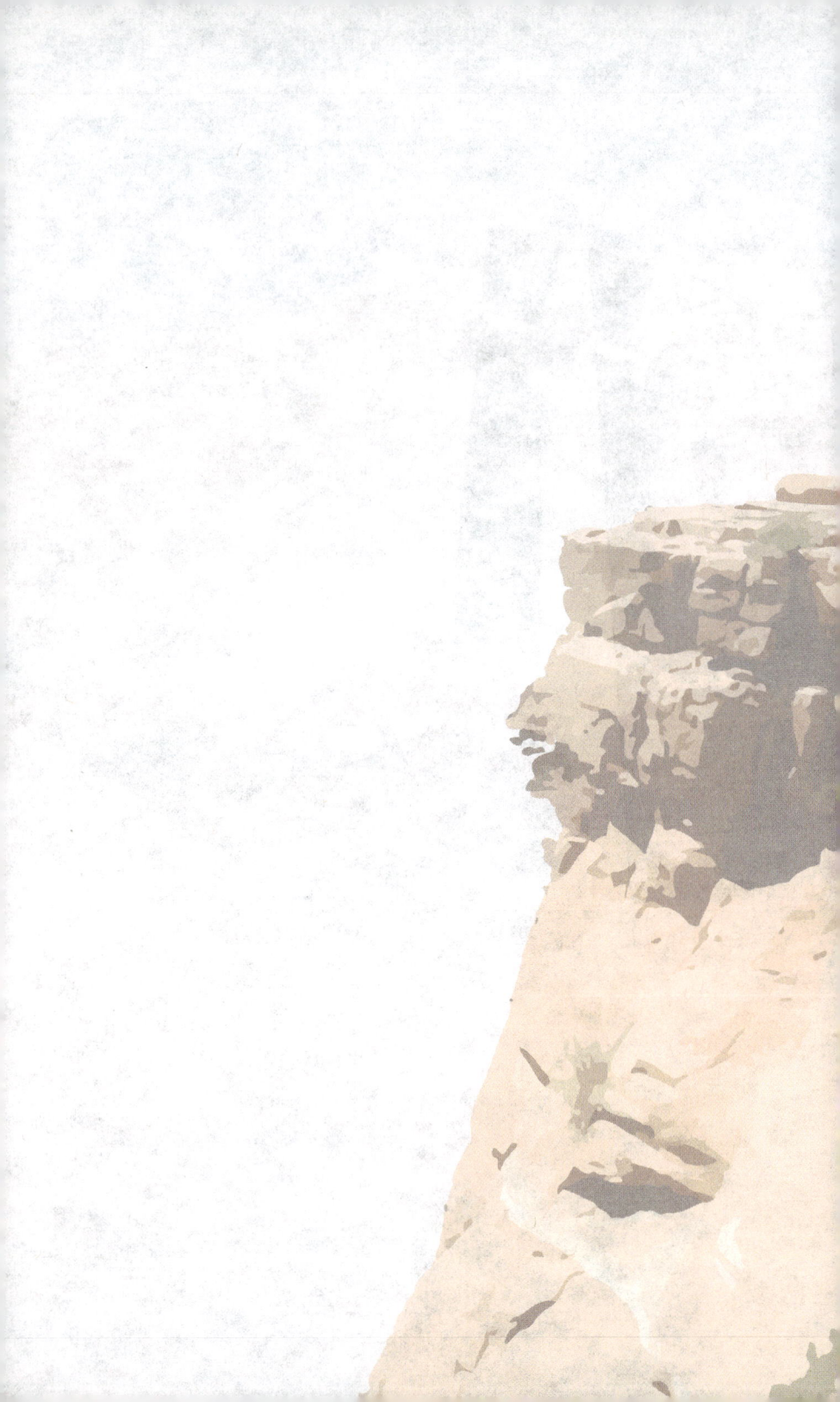

CHAPTER 2

WHERE'S MY MAP?

> *If any of you lacks wisdom, you should ask God, who gives generously to all without finding fault, and it will be given to you.*
>
> ~ James 1:5

It's about me! Write that down. Underline it. Highlight it. Bold it. Now write this down: *I am not the priority!* Underline it. Highlight it. Bold it.

Life is about you. It's about me. It's about them. We are put in a large space—earth—and given free will. Free will is the amazing ability to be able to make a choice. You control your actions, thoughts, and words. Every day you choose to either accept God into your life as a priority by letting Him walk you down the path, or you continue on your journey in life and hope *He's* following *you*. Sometimes you talk to Him, call out for Him, pray, meditate, or sing . . . you know He's there. Isn't that enough? You're a good person who believes in Jesus; that's an automatic pass into heaven, right? If God is good, He certainly would not send a good person to hell to burn. He'd never turn away a child from the gates of heaven, would He? What about the people who never have the chance to know Him because of their culture or lifestyle? Look what an impact you've made on the world, on people in society . . . everyone thinks you're a good-hearted person; of course you're living according to God's plan! Right?!

There is something so much bigger, and I look forward to the day when you discover it. It's essential to live with God as your priority and use yourself to spread His word and make a difference. This is such a difficult thing for many to understand because they feel like they are already living in God's will if they are doing good on earth; however, it's not necessarily true. Doing good deeds does not necessarily mean you're following the path God intended. While you're certainly not going to be punished for doing good, it doesn't mean you will be rewarded either. We cannot buy our way into heaven. Your desires should not be your priority. The more you focus on your own desires, the more time you spend avoiding peace. If you want peace, then you must change. If you have to call out to God and ask Him if He's there, then He's not a priority. If you stop on your trail to look for Him, then He's not a priority. Priorities are FIRST, and God should be leading you on your path DAILY—every second, every minute is about Him because you're a follower of Him! Putting Him as a priority doesn't just mean reading the Bible every day or praying before you go to bed. It's more; it's so much more. He wants you to follow Him and let Him guide you. Although you cannot physically see Him, you need to have faith that He's always in front of you and because He's good, He'll always lead you in a direction that's purposeful and meaningful. Your eyes may deceive you, but God will never fail you.

When you were born, you came prepackaged with everything you would need for your journey. On your hike you made decisions that ultimately affected the conditions of your trail. Perhaps you ignored your intuition, quit your job, and are now low on money. That changed the conditions of your trail. Sometimes it's for the better; sometimes not. Either way, now you must make adjustments. Don't think of it as an obstacle; it is just life. You deal with it and move on, taking the wisdom of each problem with you but leaving the problem behind. We've all heard it said, "To know where you're going, you have to know where you've been." The good news is you already know! It's your past! Your past is important to understanding your present, and your present is important to plan for the future. Positive or negative, your past was the past! Learn to live in the present, here and now. Once again, you can't move forward if you're constantly looking back. However, if you keep your past in the back of your mind and your focus on your next step, then you will learn to take the next step more quickly and easily because of something you've learned previously. God is so creative and has so much for you if you keep moving! Every day brings a new day . . . a new opportunity . . . a new lesson. Each day you concentrate on the past, you miss today's lesson. It's impossible to think two thoughts at the same time.

The hardest part of the journey is realizing you're physically alone on the hike. Sure, there are other people in the vicinity, there's always God, and there are signs to point you in the right direction, but NONE of them will help you if you don't first realize that no one else has trod your path. Others may intersect your path, but everyone begins at a separate trailhead. Your scenery and distance will be different, and you may have to turn around to get different gear because of unexpected weather. Things happen! Things are happening at this very second. Although two people may go through a similar circumstance such as illness, both experience different feelings because they walk separate trailheads (backgrounds).

We have all experienced negative emotions, but I promise you that if you hold onto them, you cannot move forward. Throw away your problems—it's the best thing you can do to reach peace. How are you going to rest, relax, and breathe a sigh of relief if you're carrying around extra weight and never try to start over? You have to start fresh (meaning, let go of past negative emotions) to have a new life. How do you expect to feel happy, content, and totally at peace with yourself if you think and act the opposite? You have to "walk the walk." You can't put new items in a bag that's already full. They'll just spill out.

Only you can help or hurt yourself. You're exactly where you are because of your choices. Understand that I'm speaking of your mind, not your location. However, your mind most definitely determines your location.

Do you view the cup as half full or half empty? I don't believe the correct answer to optimism is half full. It depends what you're doing with the cup. Are you drinking the liquid in it? If so, the cup is half empty. If you're filling the cup, it's half full.

WHERE'S MY MAP? 53

This is life! Sometimes you give, and sometimes you receive. Life isn't going to always be half full. This is the problem in my opinion—not that life has difficulties and obstacles but that people expect this concept of half full. See things positively, keep a good attitude, go to church, pray, be nice to others, love your neighbor, and then good things will happen, right?

Who said that? Who promised you that if you do everything according to the Bible or according to society's rules, then good things would come your way on earth? You didn't read that in a Bible—unless it was omitted in mine. In my Bible, I've read about Naomi, Joseph, Moses, and Job. These are men and women who went through hardships just as we do.

Job was a blameless man who had trust like no other. He did no evil and was one of the greatest men among the people in the East; yet his children were murdered, his fields set on fire, and his cattle stolen. As if that weren't enough, the devil inflicted sores from Job's feet to the top of his head.

In Job 3:11–26, Job asks a question that cannot be answered from earth.

> "Why did I not perish at birth, and die as I came from the womb? . . . What I feared has come upon me; what I dreaded has happened to me. I have no peace, no quietness; I have no rest, but only turmoil."

God brought Job out of suffering. Not immediately, but after suffering had occurred. Later, Job was blessed with twice as much as he had before. The Lord blessed him by giving him more donkeys, oxen, camels, and sheep. He had seven sons and three daughters. Job lived a very long life and saw four generations of his family grow up. Although many hardships faced Job, he never lost faith. During the most difficult times, Job's wife asked him, "Are you still maintaining your integrity? Curse God and die!" Job replied, "You are talking like a foolish woman. Shall we accept good from God, and not trouble?" (Job 2:9-10).

Job knew of the most important pieces of information about God. Just because you believe doesn't mean trouble will not find you. Illness, anger, disaster, loss, and disappointment found Job, and despite prayers and the negative people around him, he continued to believe that God had a plan and would lead him out of despair. He never lost faith, but he did experience disappointment and an overwhelming sense of sadness. He questioned God and wanted to die.

Moses, leading thousands of people into a land that God promised was full of good things, had limited food and water, and was instructed by God to take over cities with very strong armies. Do you think it would be easier if you heard God tell you what to do? It's no easy task to go against an enemy known for being strong. It's difficult to have a weak army and believe you can overtake a strong one, since the odds are not in your favor. Many followers believed it was best and easiest to return to Egypt rather than continue toward the Promised Land. The men repeatedly complained to Moses about their hardships, and eventually God told them they would never enter the Promised Land (since they had grumbled against Him). Even Moses would never enter the land but would spend forty years wandering around in the desert with the people. Moses questioned God:

> He asked the Lord, "Why have you brought this trouble on your servant? What have I done to displease you that you put the burden of all these people on me? Did I conceive all these people? Did I give them birth? Why do you tell me to carry them in my arms, as a nurse carries an infant, to the land you promised on oath to their ancestors? Where can I get meat for all these people? They keep wailing to me, 'Give us meat to eat!' I cannot carry all these people by myself; the burden is too heavy for me. If this is how you are going to treat me, please go ahead and kill me—if I have found favor in your eyes—and do not let me face my own ruin."
>
> ~ Numbers 11:11–15

Moses and his followers not only questioned the hardships, but the followers also didn't trust that God would take care of them in the desert. They became angry at times and let the situations, rather than faith, control their thinking. They never learned patience, but Moses always had good intentions and was a great leader because of it. God did answer Moses' prayers, and he did find peace, but the plans that God had for Moses were different than the plans that Moses had for himself.

Joseph, son of Jacob, faced his own hardships too. After being sold by his brothers for twenty shekels of silver to Ishmaelites going to Egypt, the brothers went home and convinced their father that wild animals had devoured him. They didn't like that

Joseph had dreams of ruling over them, nor the fact that their father favored him. However, God was with Joseph.

Joseph was put in charge of an Egyptian master's household. The master's wife tried several times to sleep with Joseph, but he rejected her. This angered the woman, so she lied and said Joseph had tried to sleep with her, and the accusation sent Joseph to prison. His master could have executed him, but he likely knew Joseph was not guilty.

Why did God allow such deceit and evil to be present in Joseph's life? Joseph did nothing to deserve the accusation or be sent to prison, but it happened! Why didn't God stop it?

Joseph had visions he did not understand, and they were all a part of something much bigger than he could have ever imagined. He wasn't meant to understand them when they first appeared, because undoubtedly, he would have tried to interfere. God's work is already perfect. The things that happened to Joseph were not negative but were instead steps to make him into the leader he was meant to be! Sometimes negative situations are to help humble us and provide us experiences that will assist in making us into something much greater!

Why would men destined for such great things be put in the path of deceit? Lies? Hatred? Illness? Hunger? They were all believers! They prayed! Why? Why did God let these hardships fall on them? The answer is easy, and it was written for you in the Bible, as are all the answers.

Joseph, son of Jacob, answered these questions in Genesis 45:4-8.

"I am your brother Joseph, the one you sold into Egypt.

And now, do not be distressed and do not be angry with

yourselves for selling me here, because it was to save lives that God sent me ahead of you. For two years now there has been famine in the land, and for the next five years there will be no plowing and reaping. But God sent me ahead of you to preserve for you a remnant on earth and to save your lives by a great deliverance. So then, it was not you who sent me here, but God. . . ."

God has a way of making everything work out. Where would the world be had these hardships *not* fallen on these men? Great things ended up happening to people who could have given up. It would have been easier for them to give up. As humans, we'd understand if they had lost faith in God. No "good God" would inflict painful sores on a person, leave people lost in the wilderness for forty years, or send an innocent man to prison. So why did these things happen? The answer is simple.

God didn't do those things. The devil inflicted sores on Job, the Egyptian master sent Joseph to prison, and the followers of Moses had little faith when nothing went according to their plan. God allowed the hardships to happen, and perhaps it was part of His overall plan the entire time. If Joseph hadn't been sold and hadn't gone to prison, then he would never have become second in command to Pharaoh, the ruler of Egypt. He wouldn't have been able to save his family by giving them food. Perhaps Joseph lived a life that was perfectly planned. Although he had gone through suffering and disappointment, it was all for the greater good.

These men never lost faith, but they questioned God. It's okay to question why your life is taking drastic turns, but you should never believe that God cannot bring you out of your troubles. He can, and He will—all you have to do is ask. There will always be trouble and evil in the world. God *can* interfere (we refer to these situations as miracles), but often He doesn't because every person on the earth has free will, one of the greatest gifts given to us. He allowed Adam and Eve to sin. He put the tree of knowledge of good and evil in the middle of the garden. However, He gave them control over their choices and only one rule—do not eat from the tree of knowledge. So why did God put the tree there, anyway?

We cannot control everything. You didn't create the earth; therefore, you cannot understand everything about it. As Job questions God about why He let things happen, God's response is perfect and one we all need to remember:

> Have the gates of death been shown to you? Have you seen the gates of the deepest darkness? Have you comprehended the vast expanses of the earth? Tell me, if you know all this. What is the way to the abode of light? And where does darkness reside? Can you take them to their places? Do you know the paths to their dwellings? Surely you know, for you were already born! You have lived so many years! Have you entered the storehouses of the snow or seen the storehouses of the hail, which I reserve for times of trouble, for days of war and battle? . . . Can you bring forth the constellations in their seasons or lead out the Bear with its cubs? Do you know the laws of the heavens? Can you set up God's dominion over the earth?
>
> ~ Job 38:17–33

God doesn't stop there. He keeps going. Can a human argue it . . . any of it? No. We have no control over it, and we never will. God is not telling Job this to be arrogant or to puff up His feathers and show authority. God is humbling Job. Aren't we all so small in such a big world? Why, as humans, do we feel entitled to understand and know everything? This world is not ours, nor is anything in it. God created us out of nothing, and to nothing we will return without Him.

Job's humble reply to God is, "I am unworthy—how can I reply to you? I put my hand over my mouth. I spoke once, but I have no answer—twice, but I will say no more" (Job 40:4–5).

You don't have nearly enough knowledge to understand why things happen. We can barely understand how electricity and technology are possible, let alone how the entire world is made (in detail). In one lifetime most people will study one particular skill (science, math, English, fitness, and so on). One human does not have enough time or knowledge to understand, in fine detail, everything in existence. God does, though. He created it.

Knowledge. It can be both a curse and blessing. Haven't you ever said to yourself, "I wish I didn't know that" or "I'd be better off having never gone there or heard that or done that"? Free will is the reason we often have to ask ourselves, "Where's God?" because we often don't understand how God could let evil happen in the world. Sometimes it's undeniable evil, while other times it's something we just consider negative. Why does God let the assassin go into the school and shoot multiple people? Why does He allow terrorists to set bombs off? Why does He allow tragic happenings in a church? Free will is not an easy thing to understand, nor do I believe the entire realm of free will can be understood. God doesn't control our minds or interfere with everything we do. If He allowed only "good" to enter the world, then that wouldn't be "free will." We would be robots and programmed to do only what was "good." God would be controlling us. God created everything and made everything perfect; therefore, everything is perfect . . . except one thing . . . our choices, which are under our own *free will*. God doesn't control you—*you* control you. Free will can be our flaw, if we let it be.

Life is about you. Why are you here? You are the only one with the answer to that question, and it takes soul-searching. Some call it a mid-life crisis (a suggestion that you're guaranteed something—in truth, mid-life for some people may be ten years old). Once you discover "who" you are and why you were put on the earth, your work has just begun, and it only finishes in death. Every day you will need to remind yourself why you choose to think and behave the way you do. Every day you will be given reasons to give up faith. It's easy to give up on something you can't see or hear; after all, our senses are what guide us on earth. We are used to following them. Faith is different. It's a belief and therefore is not tangible. It's a risk, but one worth taking!

Choose to be done with the past and focus on the present. Choose to see the cup for what it is in each circumstance. Your life is so unique, so special—but it's meaningless unless you make something of it. You decide what photo ops to take and how many people are going to be in your life. If you sit and stay inactive, you will lead an inactive life. Although nothing is impossible with God, you can't write a book without picking up a pen. A marathon cannot be completed without a first step. It's impossible to skydive without making the choice to jump from the plane. The decisions we make have either a positive or a negative effect on our future.

Yes, God will give you things you've not deserved. You don't deserve eternal life. You've most definitely not been deserving of every blessing in your life; however, God has a plan for you and does everything to try to help you choose His way. Free will, unfortunately, can be the reason we don't achieve God's plan.

Perhaps your destiny is to be a paramedic. Maybe God has a plan for you to save lives, be inspirational, and give hope to those who feel hopeless. Maybe you would be the last person a young boy looks at as he tightly holds your hand and says he's scared to die. You might be the person who holds on to his trembling hand, tells him Jesus will take care of him, and makes him realize there is nothing to fear. Your actions might be what inspire another to become a doctor who ultimately creates a cure for AIDS. God has a plan—a great plan. But what happens if the person refuses to go to class because drinking sounds better? What if the paramedic let negativity control his emotions the day he held the young boy's hand? God doesn't make mistakes, but people do.

Perhaps the paramedic was rude and mean to a patient, and that was what inspired the future doctor to want to change the medical world. God can use us even when we are negative because He's in complete control. What if the future paramedic knew he was being drawn to emergency medicine but decided it was "easier" and more profitable for him to take over the family business? I believe God will keep calling him back to medicine, but God isn't going to sign a paramedic license and hand it to the guy when he wakes up. You have to work for it. Yes, God will provide opportunities, He will present you with choices, and He will help you overcome every obstacle. You have to help too, though. You have to accept the gift God's given you.

Most of the time, these gifts are people. People are often our help as God provides through the hands and words of others. You pray for your aunt to walk again. God's hands work through the nurses and doctors. He gives you comfort and her strength. God mysteriously connects the organ donor with another family at exactly the perfect time. But what if the organ receiver didn't pick up the phone? What if she didn't want to receive the kidney because she thought she deserved to die from her past decision to drink too much? Is that God not providing, or the lady letting the devil overwhelm her with feelings of guilt? God answered prayers by sending the organ donor, but God didn't hand it to her Himself. He provided for His child through His other children.

You cannot progress on a trail without stepping forward. You control your own actions, and you can only progress by choosing to put one foot in front of the other. Nobody is going to lift you up and carry you to your goal, because if someone else is carrying you, you're going in *their* direction—not your own. You decide to reach your own goal. You choose whose advice to follow. You decide whether you will follow God's plan or your own.

You're unhappy because you decided to be unhappy! Everyone has something in life to be unhappy about, and while we can debate whether one situation is worse than another, it still boils down to people letting things or situations impact their way of thinking.

The world is right in front of you—what are you going to do with it? You have the capability of changing *every* situation in front of you by making a decision. Rest assured that God controls time, and what you see in front of you is purposeful. Is God trying to tell you to be a missionary? A nurse? A secretary? A writer? You were born with a certain set of unique skills. Everyone is good at something; we learned that in kindergarten too. What you choose to do with it . . . well . . . that part is completely up to you.

DAY 2, AUGUST 24, 2012: THE HEARTBEAT OF THE WILDERNESS

The sun reflected off the beautiful red rock as I arrived at Boynton Canyon Trail on Friday, August 24. Silence deafened my ears as I did a few basic stretches in the small parking lot, never taking my eyes off the distant mountains of gorgeous rusted rock and thick green trees. Excitement washed over me as I finished stretching. I was ready to find a vortex, be inspired, and write all day.

I started on the trail and let my mind immediately wander into thoughts of living in Sedona and whether or not I could handle hiking alone every day. Would I find friends easily? Could I handle being away from family? Beginning a new career? Taking a pay cut?

As I wound through the trees and narrow pathways, I was reminded of northern Michigan. Brown dirt laid a narrow path along the numerous thick green trees that were tall enough to block most of my view of the red rocks in the distance. My mind started wandering to distant memories of an ex-boyfriend. We'd had many walks in the woods, and I thought that "just maybe" he could be the one for me. He wasn't, and I don't regret my decision to end it. We were at different points in our lives. However, I couldn't help but feel that time had been wasted. I felt anger knowing that his words contradicted his actions. What he said when we first met was followed by the opposite nine months later. Irritation and regret filled my heart and left me wondering if the problem was me, him, or just the idea of us.

Turn off your mind! I shook all remaining thoughts from my head while my feet skillfully maneuvered around the fallen red rock from a nearby canyon wall. I enjoyed the sound of rock beneath my feet, the only noise for miles. I looked down at my Garmin Forerunner (a running wristband to help gauge speed and miles): one mile. I stopped to take a drink of water and admire the breathtaking views around me. Directly in front of me on the dirt trail lay a caterpillar. Its black fuzzy body was moving very slowly over the dirt in the center of the walking path. I admired the small creature for a few seconds before grabbing a stick and letting it crawl up before moving the caterpillar safely away from future hikers' feet.

As I walked away from him, I thought about God's timing. Normally, I wouldn't pay attention or be walking slowly enough to notice everything around me, but the caterpillar was a subtle reminder that I need not be in a hurry for anything. It was a reminder that no task is too small. Had I not moved the caterpillar out of the way, someone may have crushed it. Many people would say, "Who cares? It's a bug." However, I'm sure the caterpillar—future butterfly—cared. I'm not saying that it shares the same feelings we do as humans, but the point is I was able to make a difference in the *life* of a living thing. It was a reminder to slow down, take one step at a time, and help all things—no matter how pointless it may seem at the moment. The few seconds I took out of my life gave the caterpillar possibly thousands of seconds to live.

As I went further into the wilderness, I started to feel alone. I silently prayed that I'd be kept safe from any danger ahead. I decided to pick up my pace a little. Within moments a runner came from the opposite side of the path, nodding as he passed me. I smiled as he ran past and silently thanked God for the reminder that I was not alone. It was the same reminder He had used the day before. He was walking with me, and He would provide me all the reassurance and support I required.

I could feel anxiety and excitement build within my body as I neared the three-mile marker. Finally, I'd be at a vortex and feel energy like the day before! I'd be able to write and sort out my thoughts.

Just before reaching the end of the trail, I stopped again to take a drink of water. The water was refreshing in the hot sun. I glanced around and noticed a beautiful yellow butterfly that seemed to be attracted to me. It danced around me, automatically bringing a smile to my face. I didn't connect the caterpillar to the butterfly at that moment, but as I write this, I smile because I know God was showing me progression. He was showing me how things can change. The butterfly stayed by me as I hiked for the next 500 feet before it eventually disappeared into the thick trees.

Disappointment rushed over me as I climbed up fallen rock to reach the end of the trail, where I was greeted by a medium-size sign reading "END OF TRAIL." The wooden sign instructed me to go no farther. Instantly, I was displeased. The sweat dripping down my forehead had nothing to do with it, but rather, I found myself wondering where the vortex was!

I planned to spend the day writing, and I believed that I couldn't do it without a vortex! I took out my phone to try to search online for the vortex on the trail, but there was no signal. I could feel my heart rate increase as I thought about a coyote coming out from the trees. Nobody would ever find me. Nobody would hear me scream.

I stared at the sign for a while before my attention was directed to a small stack of rocks on a part of the canyon that was sticking out. I looked below the canyon and knew it was a steep drop, but the red rock was big and stable—unless I were to slip. I decided to risk it and found myself skillfully stepping across the rock and sitting down on the edge of the canyon, overlooking the trees and red rocks in the distance. Was this the vortex? I got out my pad of paper and pen and tried to concentrate on my writing. I was unable to concentrate on anything but a coyote. What if something approached me from the backside? I'd fall into the canyon from fear, or I'd be eaten!

So many thoughts were going through my head that I finally decided that I needed to turn around and retrace my steps once again. Maybe go back to the tree that I was at on the first day? I couldn't understand why God directed me to this path—there was clearly nothing here. Surely He didn't want me to come to the trail just for a caterpillar and butterfly.

I decided to run back. I only slowed down crossing small creeks and when the path became rocky. About an hour later, I found myself in an intersection that was filled with signs. Why hadn't I seen this on the way in? One sign read "Boynton Canyon Vista" with an arrow pointing to the left. I paused to study the area.

I hadn't even noticed it coming in! Should I go? As I tossed the idea around in my head, I heard the faint sound of a flute coming from the direction of the trail. Entranced by the beautiful sound, I turned down the dirt path. As I climbed over the red rocks, my attention became focused on a man sitting on the top of a high cliff.

He sat Indian style and held the flute to his mouth. I could hear him whisper out the name of the song before playing. I couldn't take my eyes off of him, I knew I was staring, but I didn't care. As I reached the top of the area, I looked up at the boulders he had climbed. How did he ever manage to climb up the rocks? There was no clear path. He gave me a slight wave as he surely noticed me staring at him. I waved back and smiled. THIS is where God wanted me to go . . . it wasn't the six-mile hike I had just completed. Had I just taken one step at a time from the beginning and thought about what was in front of me rather than the

destination or the future, then I would have reached the area more than two hours earlier.

I sat down by a twisted tree and tried to take in every inch of the beautiful area, including the thick, lush green trees, the red mountains, the cacti, the hikers, and the silence. Putting it all as a memory, I closed my eyes to pray.

Dear God, hear my prayer.

Do I belong here? Is Sedona my home? I'm confused, and I need Your help. I need You to show me the way... give me guidance... a sign... please be here with me and help me find the answers to the questions I ask. I fully admit I do not know what I'm doing. I need clear direction in my life, and I need Your help in finding it. Why am I so attracted to Sedona? I feel at peace here, but how do I know if this is right? Am I running from life at home, or am I being called here? Please continue to be with me.

Amen.

I had no desire to move, and I had no plans to do so. This was exactly where I was supposed to be! A few minutes later, the music ended. I watched the older, athletic man climb down the cliff. With amazing skill, he remained erect as he stepped carefully from rock to rock until he made it safely to the even landing where I sat. I smiled at him as he neared.

"You make beautiful music," I said in complete sincerity.

"Thank you. I have something for you," he said, producing a heart-shaped rock. The heart was clearly handmade from the rusted red rocks of the mountains. "This is from me to you. This heart is to remind you that you do not have to be in Sedona to have everything it offers. Take the heart with you and keep it as a reminder of what's here."

I thanked him and watched him walk down the rocks. He stopped two hikers coming up and produced two more hearts for them. I heard him say to the girl, "Did you see the hearts in the trees as you walked up the trail?"

I looked down over the trees as he became smaller and smaller on the trail. I could see him pointing up at the trees to the hikers. What hearts? I decided to take a mental note and look on my way out . . . but for now, I was perfectly comfortable on the small lookout! I climbed halfway up the boulders to where the flutist had been sitting, and wrote . . . and wrote . . . and wrote. The writing was in sections and clearly not a piece of any individual book. I was writing parts of many books. I stayed in the same place for more than eight hours, meditating and, well, writing!

At dusk the man came back with his flute. He made a comment about me still being in the area, and we engaged in a small conversation. He had moved to Sedona and played his flute several times a day. As he finished playing and walked away, I felt a strong desire to follow him. I wanted to be a part of his peace! I wanted to know his secret! Instead, I wrote about it because that's ultimately what God was telling me to do.

On my way out I found myself smiling. There were dozens and dozens of hearts placed carefully on the high and low branches of the trees. I shook my head. I was so focused on getting to a vortex, getting finished with the hike, that I hadn't noticed all of these hearts! I had not taken time to just enjoy the small things in life. I had no heart!

I have always cared about people, but my eyes were only concentrated on the million thoughts in my mind, and I surely wasn't enjoying the scenery around me! Wow—what I would have missed if I hadn't learned to slow down, take one step at a time, and enjoy the present.

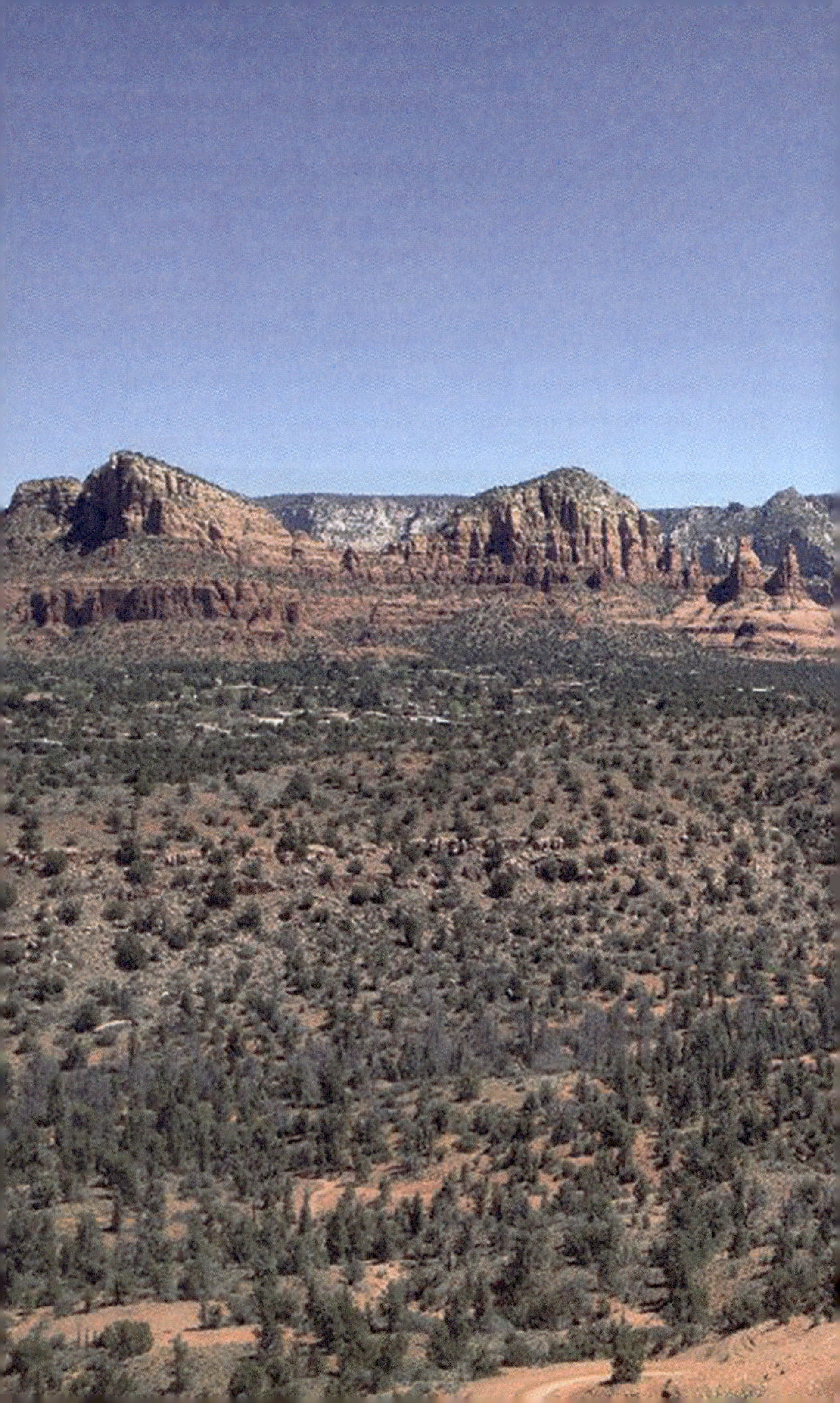

. . . OUR HEARTS, WHEN FILLED WITH THE HOLY SPIRIT, TELL US WHEN WE ARE CALLED TO DO SOMETHING. IT'S OUR MOST PRECIOUS GIFT FROM GOD—OUR LIFELINE TO HIM ON A SPIRITUAL LEVEL . . .

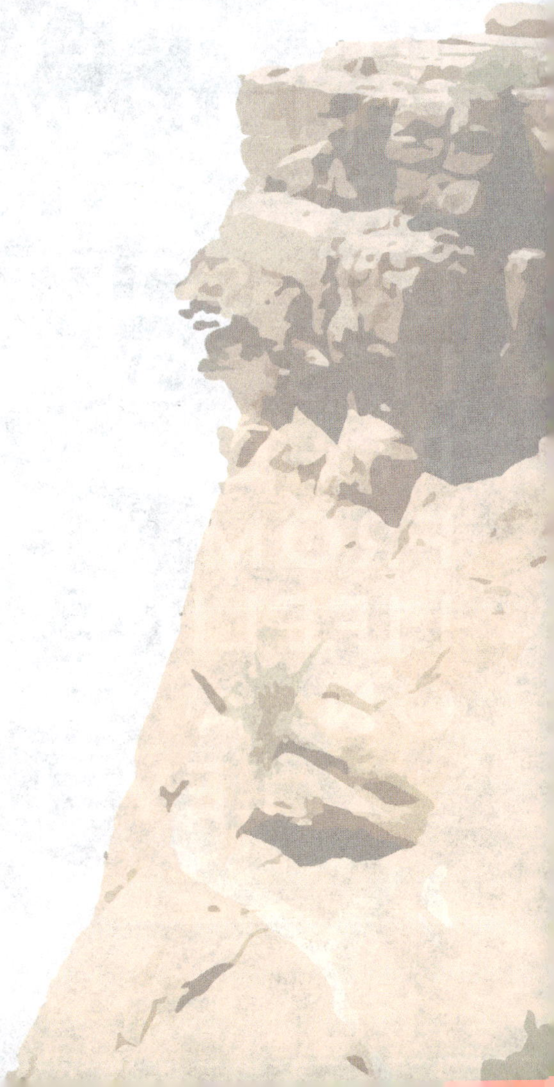

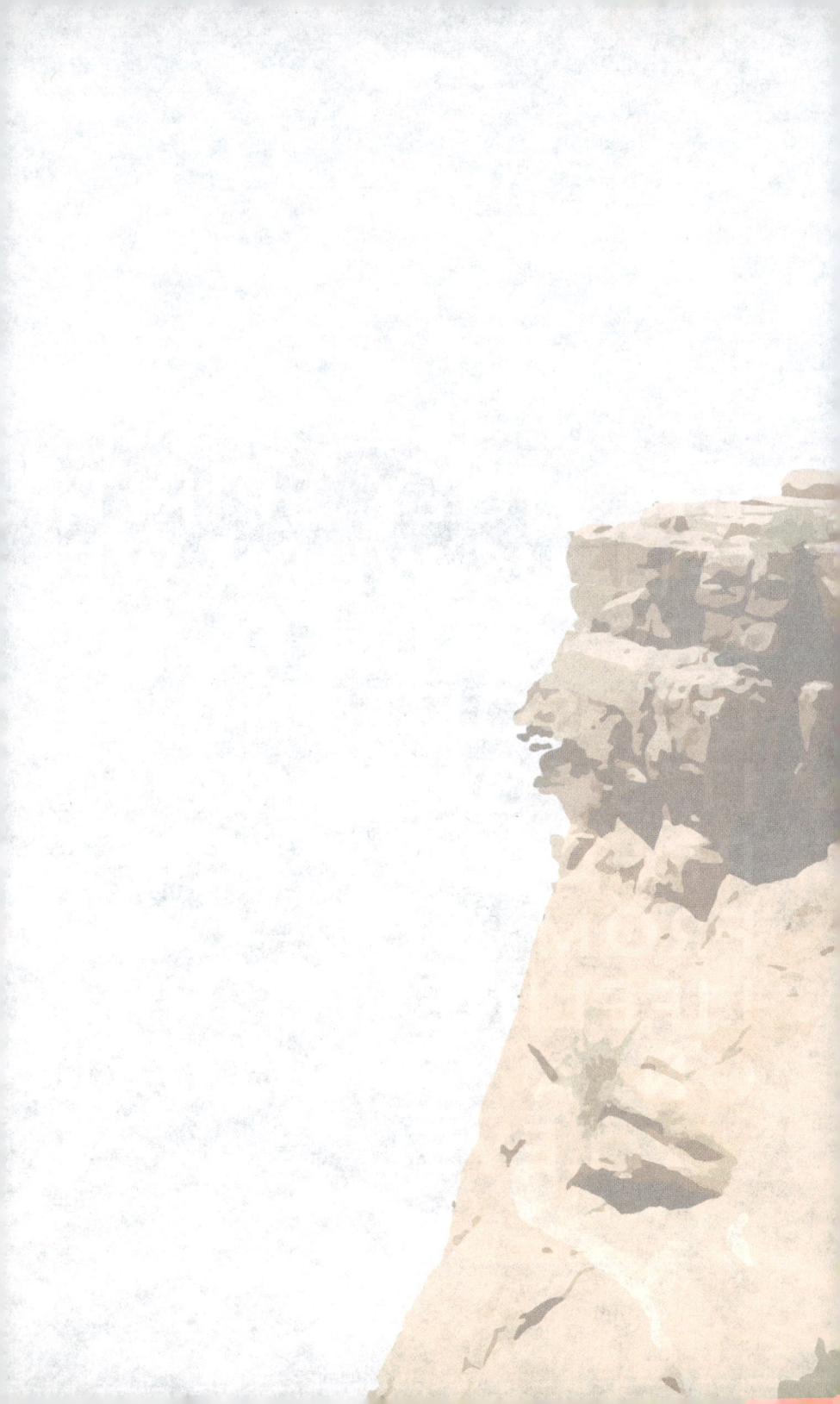

CHAPTER 3

LEFT OR RIGHT?

I will instruct you and teach you in the way you should go;
I will counsel you with my loving eye on you.

~ Psalm 32:8

    It's my personal belief that not everyone ends up living life the way God intended. With free will, sometimes our choices and God's intentions don't add up. While bad results don't necessarily mean it wasn't God's plan, I do believe that God puts things in our path to try to get us back on the original path—especially after we've made a wrong turn or decision. At one point in your life, you likely chose a path that led you in a direction you may have considered bad or wrong. At some point, you followed another person because it was safer . . . because you didn't feel confident . . . because you needed reassurance. Sometimes we choose the wrong people to let into our lives, sometimes we choose not to reach out to the person in need, and other times we are simply focused on ourselves. We are humans and have these flaws.

I don't know if we are entitled to these faults, but I believe every situation can have a positive outcome. God is always providing you an opportunity to make your life a positive experience. You may ultimately choose an option different from God's choice for you, but you always gain something from the results, and He ALWAYS tries to guide you to the place He wants you to be. If you have the potential to gain knowledge from everything, then I don't believe anything in life can be a mistake. It's a new path. It's a new direction and a potentially new perspective, if you let it be.

You desire an answer or peace within yourself, don't you? My past experiences will not help you find it, but your past will. What you are questioning in your life is a result of something that happened to you in the past. You question whether or not to get married because you've read about, seen, or been through a divorce, or maybe you've just seen some people live very unhappily together. Maybe you question whether or not to continue a particular friendship. If you have never seen hurt or been hurt in a friendship, you'd never question it. You struggle with the emotions of losing weight because at some point you or someone close to you experienced failure. You feel defeated with finances because you've had trouble with money or know someone who has. You struggle with health because you've seen the knowledge of doctors fail. You are scared of trusting because someone deceived you. Your past led you to the place you are today. Sometimes your past will guide you *away* from things, and sometimes it will guide you *to* things.

Our hearts, when filled with the Holy Spirit, tell us when we are called to do something. It's our most precious gift from God—our lifeline to Him on a spiritual level. God doesn't make incorrect decisions, and He's filled with love. Our heart is an amazing organ that gives us intuition and allows us to hear the word of God without ever picking up a Bible. It doesn't mean this is all we need, but it's the seed that needs to be watered and fed—it's the trailhead to a potentially amazing journey. It's the ability to just "know" without a greater understanding of why. The heart should never be feared, for God is good. Guilt, fear, sadness, anger, and resentment—they are in the mind, and the physical world creates them through free will. Free will is unfortunately capable of good and evil. I can *choose* to do the right thing, or I can *choose* to do the wrong thing.

Basic religion will teach you that God is good, and Satan is evil. As life takes you into building relationships through time, we tend to remember God is good but forget free will and the devil. As these relationships continue over the years, they are filled with triumphs and disappointments. Every relationship has a high and low. In life, that's what we can expect because free will makes each person unique, and that's exactly what our Creator intended. From the first sentence in the Bible, God showed creativity.

Why, with such a creative designer, do we desire to be like our neighbor? Our society puts its focus on style, such as the way we look, the way we act, what we own, etc. Imagine if we were not judged by clothing . . . if nobody looked twice at your hair . . . if money did not exist . . . if we did everything for ourselves and as a favor to another person . . . imagine a world where every person made the same decision. *GOD is much more creative!*

Free will, the most creative thing we have been given, leaves *every* moment as an opportunity. We have the ability to choose our own path and change the world. One person *can* change the world! You were born with a unique talent that was intended to be shared with the world. Quiet your mind and feel it; then life can begin. Free will was not created so we can feel disappointment, guilt, or sadness. We feel those things so the devil can stop us from achieving greatness and cause us to ignore faith and hope. The devil attacks when we are vulnerable and lack faith and hope. When we question God, when we expect one thing and get another, that's when these feelings are created.

Think about the mother who loses her child to a drunk driver, the single father raising daughters because his wife walked out, the family that has a child with special needs, the boy who was left paralyzed after a boating accident, the parents who die from a natural disaster and leave multiple children orphaned, the family that struggles for food each month, the old man battling brain cancer, or the young boy who was severely burned by his father. Is one situation worse than another? We ask God, "Why? How can good people go through such bad things?"

The answer is not within me, your pastor or priest, or your therapist. It's in you. Find the answer by reading the Bible and having faith. It requires time, not a location (such as a vortex) or money. You may think you don't have time to read the Bible, but you have to *make* time to read about the trials that every great leader went through, the losses they endured, the countless times they felt as if God were testing them. There's nothing you have experienced in life that has not been written. I've not come across a time in the Bible where a person who had faith, full faith, did not overcome each hurdle in front of them. Once again, bad things happen to good people, even in biblical times, and they will continue to happen. There are just some things we do not understand and cannot comprehend because we are limited in knowledge. We are so small in a big world, and while our problems seem so big, they are quite the opposite. Your problems are no greater than your neighbors'. The ninety-year-old man battling cancer will never fully understand the four year old with leukemia because, although the situations are similar, they are unique to each person and have the ability to teach different things to all involved.

While it's true you may have more hardships than those around you, it's not true that you have it worse than anyone else. Each person can debate why his or her life is harder than another's. We do not possess the knowledge to understand everything about our own lives, so why try to understand time, intuition, illness, natural disaster, or death? We cannot fully understand "good," so why should we know bad? It's impossible to know where life will take us because each person is responsible for the creativity of his/her own path through free will.

God does not leave you alone on the hike but connects with you through the Holy Spirit. Don't let your mind fool you into ignoring that feeling . . . the one you can't explain . . . the one that leads you to rely solely on faith. It's the feeling that tells you to avoid the dark alley at night; it's not fear but intuition. The feeling that tells you to stay even when you feel like going, to laugh when you feel like crying, to love when you have every reason to hate, to forgive when there is no repentance, to give when you have little to share, to help when there is no time, to share when there is only one to receive, to listen when you're busy, to be strong when you feel weak, to tell a secret that shouldn't be silenced, to provide and get nothing in return, to trust beyond past experience, to go from crawling to running, to take the chance when odds are against you, to see beyond what is in front of you, and to hear the silent, unspoken words. These are the opportunities that make a difference and change the world! We all have purpose that's only obtained through the choices we make. Do you choose to live life or live through life?

The rainbow is a promise from God that He will never again destroy the earth by water. He has more promises too. He promises eternal life for those who accept Jesus Christ as their Savior. He promises to listen when we pray. He promises that He has a plan for you if you listen. He promises that earth will bring you disappointments and turmoil but that light will always overcome darkness. God promises never to leave you alone and that there is nothing that He cannot overcome.

Free will.

A caring Father.

Light.

Love.

Eternal Life.

Perhaps life doesn't seem so bad after all, huh? We make it hard, though, on a daily basis. We are filled with desires, selfishness, and thoughts that may lead us to justify sin. We believe that because we have grown up in a different generation with a different society that we will be excused from following the instructions of the Bible. We justify sin by calling God a "loving God" who wouldn't punish "good-hearted" people. Society caters to sin by giving second chances, allowing people to buy themselves out of trouble, and overlooking certain things depending on a relationship or job connection.

The people in the New Testament didn't have dinner with Moses or Abraham or David. They didn't even know them personally. Their way of "growing up" was completely different from how Moses and Abraham lived. It wasn't a span of just a hundred years or so. They were thousands of years apart. Now we live thousands of years apart from them, and we feel entitled to *exceptions* because it's a "new world," a different way of living.

Today our sins typically don't include worshipping idols or burning down temples, but we live in a society where adultery is common. Judgment is all too common in the world by Christians and non-Christians alike. As a majority, we don't honor the Sabbath or follow all of the Ten Commandments on a daily basis. We live in a country where competition and rising to the top is encouraged and the only way to make a better than average living. We envy those who have more than we do, and some people do anything to get ahead, including pushing others down. Some Christians go to church each week but are some of the most unreligious people you will ever meet. Likewise, there are many people who claim to be Christians but judge the church, other members, and question the Word of God without ever having read the Bible. As Christians, we should be living as an example to everyone without judgment. We should be knowledgeable about the Bible because Christianity is built upon it. Although there are various ways to interpret parts of the Bible, there are many sections that are easily understood.

> The cashier forgets to charge you for the water beneath your cart. You don't realize it until you get home. Do you turn around and pay for it, or do you justify why it is okay to keep it (in other words, steal it)? She forgot; it's not your fault, you tell yourself. They've overcharged you before, so it all evens out. Surely you won't go to hell for stealing! It's not like you did it on purpose!

The rich neighbor who refuses to associate with you because you're "beneath her" is now stranded on the expressway because her tire went flat. Do you stop? Maybe you silently smile and say, "Karma is sweet." You know *someone* will stop eventually, so why should you care?

That darn stray cat is back in your yard meowing for food or wanting to get out of the cold. You hate cats—not to mention you're allergic to them. There are so many of them in the neighborhood, and all they seem to do is breed more! Anyway, you're not going to take that cat in. It's not yours. What are you going to do, save every stray cat in the world? You can't afford to feed them all even if you tried, and, besides, you're allergic.

Your husband . . . ugh . . . he doesn't understand. He doesn't *try* to understand. He insists that cleaning the house is "a woman's job." He doesn't respect what you do for a living, and he can't even listen. He never makes you feel appreciated, and he puts you down every chance he gets. You never have sex anymore; the thrill is gone. Why wouldn't you think of cheating? It's not really adultery to simply "think" about it, and it's certainly not a "big" deal to flirt as long as it doesn't go any further. That's way better than that friend you have who "really" cheats on her husband. You know, the one who is physically involved with her boss. It's not really her fault, though. Her boss listened, treated her better, and actually spent time with her. Doesn't she deserve happiness?

Your unreliable friend wants you to write her a letter of reference, and then she squeezes into a dress that's three sizes too small for her and asks if it looks okay. You know she's been struggling with her weight, so you nod your head yes and hand her the reference letter where you attempted to make her negative attributes semi-positive. It's all right to lie in that circumstance. It's only your opinion, and you didn't really lie . . . you just didn't tell her the truth. Similar to when you told the boss you were late because of traffic . . . I mean, you did get caught by one red light; it wasn't a complete lie.

Honor the Sabbath? If I don't work seven days a week, I can't put food on the table. God understands that! I'm tired and I have to get up and work a twelve-hour shift. My neighbor has three kids, and she can't make it to church either, but she's a good person. She volunteers at the Red Cross and rings the Salvation Army bell at Christmas. You don't need the Bible or church to be religious. I pray every day. God will understand.

People don't wait until marriage to become intimate. Sure, they probably did in the 1800s, but times have changed. People are more open with their sexuality now, and it's okay. As long as the two of us care about each other, what's the harm? It's not like I'm a prostitute. That's different. Besides, I only slept with two people . . . it's not a lot. I know someone who sleeps with a different person each week; I don't agree with that.

Those words don't mean what you think! Using God's name with another word is not "like that." It's just an expression. People understand that I'm not really talking about God! They didn't even say those kinds of things "back then," so I know that's not what they meant by using the Lord's name in vain.

More than half of marriages fail; divorce is not a big deal.

That homeless man is a drunk; I'm not giving him anything.

Don't go near that man. He's on the sex offender list.

She is just doing her job.

LEFT OR RIGHT?

Your insurance doesn't pay for this prescription. I'm sorry . . . it's just the way the system works.

No. We can't do that; it's company policy.

She's disabled. She's not really going to know if you give her back the right amount of change.

I hit that car door with mine, but I'm surprised that other car still runs, so there's no point in leaving a note.

They live in a trailer park, so there's no reason to go to that neighborhood. They probably aren't registered voters anyway.

I know her father. Stay away from *that* family.

That drunk driver really did hit me, so I'll lie and say my neck doesn't feel right. He deserves a lawsuit since he was driving under the influence!

Your son is the quarterback of the school team? Oh, I can fix that grade.

The dog doesn't need to walk or to be played with. He has a bed and food; that's better than if he were in the pound!

It's a beer! I'm not snorting cocaine.

I'm a nice drunk.

Nobody will ever know. Just copy these answers.

That thief took my purse. I'm going to say there was $500 in there instead of $50. He deserves it anyway for stealing!

I was injured at work, but I feel better now. However, I want more time off.

Justifying sin. We've all broken the Ten Commandments in thought, word, or deed. If you consider "do not commit adultery" to be the physical act alone, you're wrong. If you think "do not murder" refers only to the physical act of killing someone, you're wrong. We murder with thoughts and words too. We are all sinners. We don't deserve heaven. We don't deserve a Savior or grace, and that's why I am so thankful that God is loving. He provides grace for us even though we don't deserve it.

Should you feel bad about your sins? YES. Should you punish yourself for the rest of your life? NO. You are already forgiven in the eyes of the Lord. Make no mistake though; we will all answer for our actions. Jesus died for us to be forgiven, not so we can keep sinning repeatedly. Repenting from sin means that you sincerely try not to do it again. It's not just a simple, "I'm sorry, Lord. Please forgive me." He knows your heart and therefore knows when you truly seek forgiveness and truly accept what His one and only Son did for you.

FREE WILL . . . the will to choose between right and wrong. Would it be easier if we knew the difference between right and wrong for sure? Wouldn't it be much easier if God just *told* us what was right and what was wrong? Can't He just be direct? Listen. God really is loving and caring but also what we modern-day people would call *blunt*. He didn't leave us in the dark about right and wrong. Isn't that great? He gave us the Light in a large book with small print—we know it as "the Bible."

DAY 3, SATURDAY, AUGUST 25, 2012: A LEAP OF FAITH

The large blue sky gave a beautiful contrast to the rusted red rocks that surrounded me on Saturday, August 25. The sun was shining perfectly to reflect the depth of the mountains that seemed endless. I walked away from my private balcony. I could feel excitement build up in my body as I put on gym pants with a thin, long-sleeved shirt. I knew today was going to be a risk. It was the only part of the four-day trip where I made a plan I couldn't back out of without losing hundreds of dollars . . . it was a leap of faith. I decided to spend a beautiful Arizona morning skydiving. I had already been once with a friend back in Michigan, but this time it was just me. I'd be lying if I said I wasn't nervous. If the money had been refundable, I might have stuck to hiking for the entire day. But it wasn't.

When I arrived after a thirty-minute drive, I signed all the necessary paperwork and watched a video to explain all the things that could potentially go wrong. It informed me that everything is man-made and subject to fail; therefore, I was taking a potentially fatal risk.

"Such is life," I thought. "Everything is subject to fail."

As I waited for the video to end, I silently reprimanded myself for not researching Red Rock Skydiving in Cottonwood. A few months prior, I had seen a video posted on Yahoo with an eighty-year-old woman whose straps were not tight enough. I'm not sure of the location where she was skydiving, but during the free fall she almost fell out and could have plunged thousands of feet to her death. Thankfully, she lived. However, as I watched the video, I made a mental note to check out the reviews on skydiving if I ever chose to go again. I had booked this particular skydiving trip spontaneously. I was watching a movie on my couch with a friend the day before I left to embark on my adventure.

"I'm going skydiving again," I had said aloud.

She looked up from the movie and nodded briefly, "Okay."

It was a normal response that any family member or friend would have given me. They were no longer shocked by my "live in the moment" personality.

My thoughts were interrupted by a voice. "You couldn't find anyone to come with you?" A tall, smiling man stepped into the room.

We had a small conversation before he introduced me to my tandem partner. I felt at ease with him too. He had thousands of jumps around the world but loved the beauty of Arizona. He told me they would fly me over Sedona as we climbed to the appropriate height, and then we would loop back around to make the jump over Cottonwood. Although I had been skydiving before, I was relieved as they went over all the equipment and preparation again. They had the same rules as Michigan, so I found myself relaxing.

"You don't have a parachute. What are you going to do?" He jokingly asked me as he videotaped us before climbing into the small airplane.

"Rely on you," I said, smiling.

"Well, you don't need a parachute to skydive; you need one to skydive twice," he joked.

As the pilot, my tandem partner, and I rode steadily up to 10,000 feet, I instantly felt calm. If God wanted to take me, He could. I looked out at the red rock formations and the Coconino Forest. The red and green landscape with a blue sky looked like a perfectly painted picture as we soared thousands of feet above. I didn't care that nobody familiar was with me. I knew God was with me. However, I also knew God was leaving skydiving in the hands of my partner. He had given him the knowledge and skills of skydiving, but things could always go wrong. I knew that just because I was on a vacation with God, things could still go badly. The parachute might not open.

"You doing okay?"

I nodded. "I'm starting to think this might be a crazy idea."

He laughed. "It is!"

I shrugged and smiled. I thought about my friend Lindsey and myself doing it a year earlier. I was more nervous the first time. Had she decided to back out, I would have left with her. She gave me courage then, and now this unfamiliar man was putting my mind at ease with his humor and sincere smile.

"We're ready," he said, motioning for me to go to the door of the plane. We pulled it open together, and he sat on the edge, motioning for me to put my arms on the chest straps and keep my head up. The wind was strong. I could feel my legs flying to the right. I paid no attention to the faint view of land below me but was only concerned with the strength of the wind. I didn't remember the wind being as strong in Michigan. The man didn't seem concerned as he pushed us out of the plane using the strength of his upper body.

I could feel my stomach slightly drop as we went free falling, 10,000 feet down, into the clear sky. The wind was strong, and I could see my skin being pulled up. I could easily breathe, and before I knew it, my partner was tapping me on the shoulders (the signal that I could release my grip from the straps and put my hands out). After a minute of falling, he pulled the parachute cord. Complete silence came over the world. After my first jump, I've thought of skydiving as a form of meditation. There's no sound that high up . . . it's a silence that cannot be experienced on earth. We floated in silence as he let me guide the parachute left and right. We landed on our feet that day, much different than when I had landed softly on my butt the first time in Michigan.

I had to wait about fifteen minutes for the video and pictures to be placed on a disc. While I waited, the manager came out and said the person after me had canceled.

"Do you want to go again?" the man asked. "I don't have anything to do. We can give you a really good deal."

I laughed. "I don't think I should press my luck." It wasn't that I didn't want to go, but I had only planned on going once, and I was excited to get to my trail.

"There's no luck in skydiving," he said, handing me my pictures and CD.

As I drove back to Sedona, I recalled his last words and considered the meaning. In life there are no guarantees and no luck either. God has provided us with everything we need on our hike. He left nothing out. By using God's resources, you will find that you don't need luck. Life advances by the choices you make using your own knowledge and the people around you and realizing that all of it is a product of God.

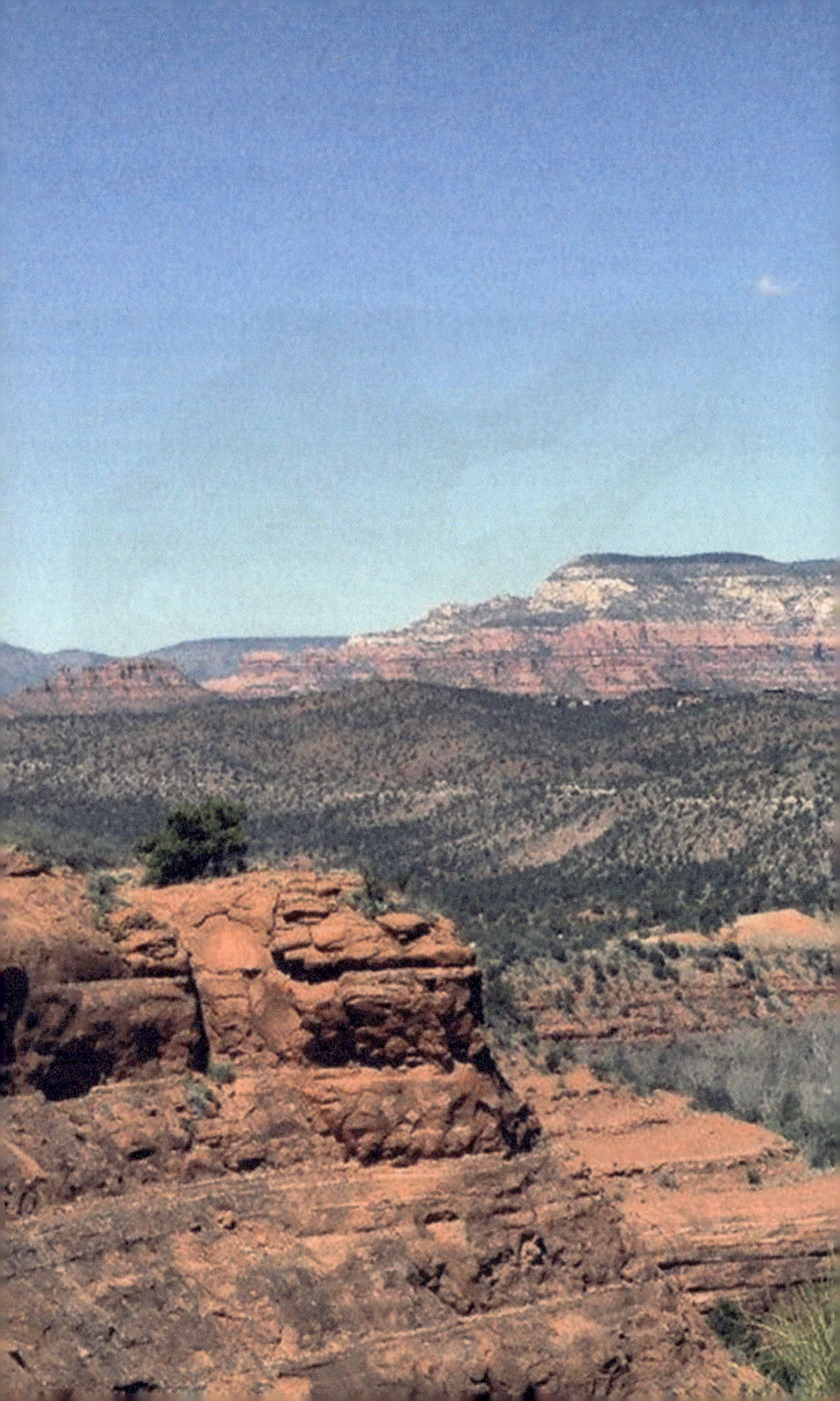

"... REMEMBER, THIS IS YOUR FEAR TRYING TO STOP YOU FROM GETTING TO THE TOP OF THIS MOUNTAIN! THERE IS SOMETHING UP THERE WAITING FOR YOU. GOD'S WITH YOU—GO!"

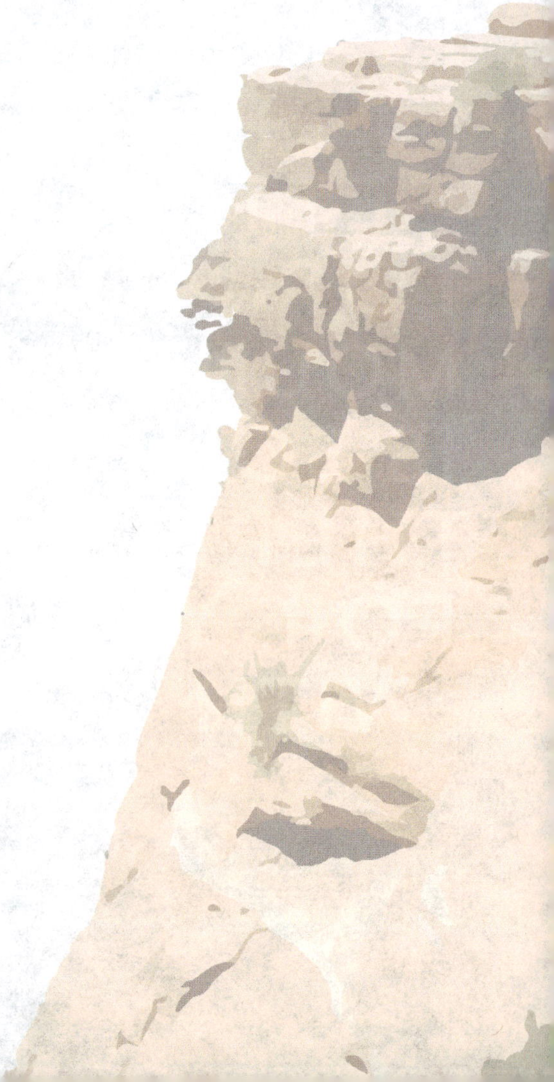

CHAPTER 4

STOP FOR DIRECTIONS

Do not boast about tomorrow, for you do not know what a day may bring.

~ Proverbs 27:1

    Life is lived by choices, and I encourage you to choose happiness. Don't wait for your goals to be magically achieved; make them happen by following God! Take the risk if God is asking, because there's nothing He will ask of you that will not lead to an improvement in your life. There's nothing to fear, for we walk in the path of the Lord with faith. Faith means He will lead you to a place of things beyond your imagination. He's most powerful, and nothing is beyond His reach. Darkness can never overcome light; therefore, believe that—through Jesus—you can do anything you imagine. Why would we be granted the ability to imagine if we don't have the ability to conquer? Without God and Jesus, we have nothing; with them, we have everything. There are no limits, except when we allow the devil to play with our mind and control our actions. With complete trust and faith in God, we should be at complete serenity and unaffected by the negativity of another person, because we know the plan for our individual self is better than the mind can bear to comprehend.

With faith, there has to be an inevitable amount of patience. We want answers now, but God doesn't answer the same as our neighbor, because God is not of this earth. He communicates through the Holy Spirit, and sometimes it can be hard to listen —and even harder to follow.

There are no unanswered prayers. God hears you. He responds—maybe not today or a month from now, but always! The answers are not always audible or visible. Our eyes and ears can fail us, but God will never send us in the wrong direction. He communicates with us daily, every second. You might *know* what you should do, but your mind finds a million reasons why you shouldn't, so you don't. Many people let emotions dictate their actions (or lack of action).

I once heard a friend, Tom, say that he disagreed with the statement, "God will never give you more than you can handle." My immediate reaction was to disagree with him, but instead I listened. He had fought off cancer and blood clots in both lungs only to be diagnosed with a second case of cancer within six months. He wasn't expected to live. The pain, hurt, and fear was more than he thought he could handle at times, both emotionally and physically. I believe God was with him, giving him hope and comfort before, during, and after his cancer and chemotherapy treatments. God gives all of us more than we can handle on a daily basis. It's through His grace that we get through a day, and it's through faith that we overcome illness. Does God give us more than we can handle? I believe life is too much for us to handle without Him. However, I believe as long as we have God, then there's absolutely nothing that is too much for us to overcome. It's okay to question your own strength, but never question God's.

God doesn't give cancer. God gives strength and courage without guarantees. Prayer doesn't always "work" the way we imagine. God answers, but it's not always the answer we had hoped for. Always trust that God knows best, even if that means life has taken a direction you did not intend. People are responsible for people. Your life is in the hands of the doctors, nurses, paramedics, and EMTs. Can God intervene? Yes. Does He? Yes. Can He hear prayers and change the outcome? Yes!

The devil will test you, people will fail, and life will take you down unexpected turns. Believe that God can and will provide you everything you need to bring you exactly to a place that gives you comfort, peace, and serenity. Live strong, but die happy. This earth is only the beginning of something so much better, if you allow yourself to open the gift God has provided; let Him lead you. He's offering this gift every second.

I'm surprised at the number of people who dismiss the Bible as unimportant. I understand that mindset because I used to have it. I already knew what the Bible consisted of—a bunch of unpronounceable names with locations I couldn't identify and the classic stories of Jonah and the whale, Adam and Eve, and David and Goliath. I didn't go to church, but I knew about these people. The Bible . . . it's that book about the Ten Commandments and how everyone knew Jesus was coming. The Bible is about Jesus and tells about His crucifixion. What more is there to know?

The Bible. A series of books about murder, sex, alcohol, salvation, grace, love, adultery, healing, temptation, anger, kindness, and betrayal. There is nothing we can experience on earth that hasn't already been covered. The Bible is an instructional book that teaches us how to deal with life. It gives us answers to things we struggle with on a daily basis. It should be the one book we study, because it's not an opinion of a licensed professional but the Word of our Creator.

It's more than hard-to-pronounce words or just stories that someone wrote down. The people and the locations within the Bible connect us with our Savior. They explain the reason He had to come. It's amazing how much the New Testament connects with the Old Testament. The Bible wasn't written in one time period but over a span of approximately 1,500 years. These aren't people who knew each other or grew up together, yet their stories are linear. The Bible is a fascinating read but isn't a book you will understand after reading it one, two, or three times. In fact, nobody will ever understand the entire Bible; however, each time you read it, your relationship with God grows.

Start reading a study Bible and learn what God has to say to you through His Word. Read what our Savior did for us in John 14:6: "Jesus answered [Thomas], 'I am the way and the truth and the life. No one comes to the Father except through me.'" If we don't know Jesus, we can't go "through" him. Knowing him is different from knowing OF him. You may know of a famous actor, but you don't really know who he/she is. Knowing someone means being familiar with their character. Do you know what Jesus did for you? What He did for others?

Jesus didn't just come to die for us. Jesus was a perfect example of how we should live! He fed the poor, comforted the weak, loved His enemies and persecutors, taught forgiveness, and most of all, He showed us that trusting in God should always be a priority. He didn't just say these things; He made Himself an example through His words, thoughts, and actions. These examples can all be part of our daily lives. Loving, teaching, comforting, and trusting in God does not cost money. These are things we are all able to do.

Jesus taught us mercy. In Matthew 9:35-36, we read, "Jesus went through all the towns and villages, teaching in their synagogues, proclaiming the good news of the kingdom, and healing every disease and sickness. When he saw the crowds, he had compassion on them, because they were harassed and helpless, like sheep without a shepherd."

Jesus taught us faith. When Pilate questioned him about being the king of the Jews, Jesus could have said "no" and saved his life, "So Pilate asked Jesus, 'Are you the king of the Jews?' 'You have said so,' Jesus replied" (Luke 23:3).

He taught us forgiveness. "Two other men, both criminals, were also led out with him to be executed. When they came to the place called the Skull, they crucified him there, along with the criminals—one on his right, the other on his left. Jesus said, 'Father, forgive them, for they do not know what they are doing'" (Luke 23:32-34).

He taught humbleness. "When he had finished washing their feet, he put on his clothes and returned to his place. 'Do you understand what I have done for you?' he asked them. 'You call me "Teacher" and "Lord," and rightly so, for that is what I am. Now that I, your Lord and Teacher, have washed your feet, you also should wash one another's feet. I have set you an example that you should do as I have done for you. Very truly I tell you, no servant is greater than his master, nor is a messenger greater than the one who sent him. Now that you know these things, you will be blessed if you do them'" (John 13:12–17).

He taught the Bible. "He said to them, 'This is what I told you while I was still with you: Everything must be fulfilled that is written about me in the Law of Moses, the Prophets and the Psalms.' Then he opened their minds so they could understand the Scriptures. He told them, 'This is what is written: The Messiah will suffer and rise from the dead on the third day, and repentance for the forgiveness of sins will be preached in his name to all nations, beginning at Jerusalem. You are witnesses of these things. I am going to send you what my Father has promised; but stay in the city until you have been clothed with power from on high'" (Luke 24:44–49).

The greatest book ever written was written just for you. The beginning of it should read, "Dedicated to all God's children," because he made each and every one of us. God used people to write it for you. If your parent, sibling, best friend, teacher, doctor, or favorite actor wrote a book and dedicated it to you, you would read it, right? How much more important is our Creator, our Father in heaven? How much more important is it to try to abide by His rules rather than society's? How much more important is it to make time for the One who created us and the One who created time?

Grow in your faith and relationship with God, but also read to grow within yourself. The Bible gives us knowledge and wisdom of God, teaches us how to live life with purpose, and provides comfort to each of us who seek it. The Bible can be everything you need it to be because it was specifically designed for "life," and there's nothing in this life that hasn't been written. On the final day, you want to be prepared. It is written in Revelation 1:7, "Look, He is coming with the clouds', and 'every eye will see Him, even those who pierced him'; and all the peoples of the earth 'will mourn because of Him.' So shall it be! Amen."

When we know a hurricane is coming, people prepare by boarding their houses or evacuating. Rain comes, and we grab an umbrella. The sun is too hot, so we put on sunscreen. The water is too deep, so we use a lifejacket. The music is too loud, so we put in earplugs. The ground is too icy, so we salt it. We spend every day preparing for the future. We prepare by going to work and saving for retirement or saving to pay the bills. We save for a vacation in the future or for college education. We work for tomorrow. However, with the single most important thing in our lives, we wait for a reason to pray, we wait for more time in our schedule, we wait for the roads to be clear so we can drive to church, and we wait for there to be some sign that the end of the world is coming.

He's not visible, but God is always here. We are not guaranteed tomorrow, nor are we promised the next second. If you believe in the Bible, then you also believe that our Savior will be back. If He comes in the next hour, are you prepared? Is this how you want Him to see you? Although He already knows our thoughts, words, and deeds, He's willing to forgive those who repent. He wants you as part of His family because He loves you. He loves you enough that He died for your sins to be forgiven.

PART II, DAY 3, SATURDAY, AUGUST 25: CLIMBING TO FAITH

After skydiving, Cathedral Rock Trail was next on my agenda. It's supposed to have a vortex and be an "easy to moderate" trail that requires good hiking boots. (My definition of an "easy to moderate" trail and Arizona's definition differ quite greatly.) I was prepared with good hiking boots, enough water, snacks, medical equipment, and a whistle as I arrived in the parking lot. In the distance I could see a very large red rock mountain formation. I had never hiked in this part of Sedona, and my initial thought was that the rust of the rocks seemed to be a brighter red.

From the parking lot, I crossed a small creek. I paused at it to admire the beauty of the clear water rushing along the red dirt and small rocks. Green trees lined the creek with the mountains seemingly smiling in the background through their branches. As I continued my walk, I made a mental note that I'd have to bring visitors back to this trail. I'd been hiking on a lot of them, but this one seemed to have something more special about it.

Within minutes of my initial hike, I reached a flat landing that had multiple trees twisted. A vortex! My attention went in front of me as my trail gave me the option of continuing a large, steep climb up the mountain. I watched the hikers climbing on all fours up the "trail." I softly shook my head. I had NO desire to go to the top of the red rocks. I was here to write and excited to feel that way without hiking six miles prior to sitting down in a vortex.

I sat next to a twisted tree and began to put my pen to paper. Every few minutes, I directed my attention back to the continued trail and the people heading up the mountain. Why couldn't I just concentrate? I really didn't care about conquering any path, but something, something inside me wanted to go to the top. I tried just to write, but with no progress, I packed up and set out on the trail that would lead me up the steep mountain.

"Go!" I had to tell myself multiple times as I was on all four limbs, sometimes feeling like I was literally holding on for my life through grooves in the rocks. There wasn't a clear path; it was just a trail marked by rocks cradled in large bins separated every fifteen feet. "This is not hiking; this is rock climbing!" I said out loud. Nobody was around me to hear me, and that made me even more nervous. If I fell, people would see me, but they would be too far away to help. I reached for the next groove in the rock and moved my feet to the slight grooves in the side of the rock as I lifted my body up. Yes, literally rock climbing but with no lines hooked to safety. My flat-leveled background in Michigan left me feeling unprepared for this "easy to moderate" Arizona trail. "Please, God, be with me" was often followed by my reminding myself, "Remember, this is your fear trying to stop you from getting to the top of this mountain! There is something up there waiting for you. God's with you—go!"

God certainly had something waiting... someone waiting. As I arrived at the top, I was on all fours and staring at the ground, thankful I could see it! My attention was immediately drawn to four shoes, two pairs. I followed the shoes up the legs, the legs to the stomachs, and the stomachs to the faces. I was greeted by a man and a woman smiling enthusiastically at me.

"You made it!" The man said, still smiling.

"Is it worth it?" I asked, grinning and struggling to get to my feet.

"Definitely," the woman answered. She seemed to study me as she watched me take my water bottle and look down at the area I had just come from.

"Great," I whispered. "I guess I should have thought about how I am going to get down!" I said. There was an undeniable sense of disappointment in my voice. I was fearful. I had so much fear, I doubt I would have gone back down the trail without the two of them being there. "How am I going to get back down?" I asked the question aloud to nobody in particular.

"You take one step at a time." The man spoke confidently with a very direct manner. "You never look beyond your next step!"

I felt energy rush throughout my body. IT'S HIM. I looked into the man's sincere eyes and immediately felt a connection to him. I can't tell you how long I looked at him.

I finally answered him. "So how much farther do I have to go to find the vortex?"

The man's smile got bigger, while the woman giggled. She continued to study me. "Honey, you're in it!"

"What? Where?"

"It's a place. You have to feel it. You didn't even have to come up here to be in it. You were in it sitting down there when you were reading."

I sighed. "Well, I guess I'll sit up here awhile and enjoy the view," I mumbled but unable to take my eyes off the older man's blue eyes.

He continued to smile. "What is your question?"

I shrugged, confused by his question. "What do you mean?"

"I mean, what's your question? You came all the way up here; what did you want God to answer?"

"Oh," I said, shocked that he knew why I had come. "Um . . . I have a ton of questions."

"The answers are all in your heart. You know that, right?" The woman chimed in.

My attention went back to her. "I have a hard time listening to it, but, yes, I know."

The man came to my side and placed a hand on my shoulder. "What's your question? I will help you learn to listen."

I nervously let out a laugh. "How much time do you have?" I asked, pointing to my wrist. I expected him to be more interested in small talk rather than sincerely wanting to know my problems.

He smiled. "Each morning, God tells me where to go, and today He told me to go on this trail at this time. I lead people. I help them find answers. I helped this lady conquer her fear, and she's up here enjoying the view now. She's right. The answer is within you—you're just not listening."

I nodded, unable to talk. IT'S HIM. I grinned. "YOU'RE the reason I came up here! I wasn't content sitting down there writing because God wanted me to meet you. He kept telling me to climb."

He nodded. "Okay, so what's your question?"

"Well, I have a lot of them . . ."

"What's the one that is on your mind right now, at this very moment?"

"How do I know when to let someone go?"

"What do you mean? Be more specific. Form it into a yes/no question."

"Is he the right one for me?"

"Okay. Ask God."

We walked over to the edge of the mountain, and I silently asked God my question.

The man's voice was soothing. "Now, what is your heart feeling? Is it blank? Is it fluttering? Are you feeling like it's a yes?"

"Well, I feel nothing, void. Then I feel my heart start to race. I think yes, then I come up with a million reasons why it's no."

"Quit thinking! Feel it. A flat, void nothing is a no. The fluttering, increased excitement is a yes. Rationalizing it is your mind."

"I can't get my mind to shut off! That's the problem," I said, feeling defeated. A part of me wanted to cry. Am I supposed to live here? What do You want me doing for a career? Why do I deserve heaven? What am I doing for other people? How do I forgive family members? How do I get over feelings of guilt? Why do I keep my schedule so packed? What am I avoiding? Why can't I feel content? Where is my peace?

"You need therapy," he said, studying my face.

I laughed at the polite statement. He didn't mean it negatively. "I go to therapy," I told him. "That's apparently not helping as much as I need it to." I made light of the conversation. "I will stay up here until I figure this out."

"Where are you staying?" he asked. "Wait, don't tell me where you're staying. Are you going to be around tomorrow? Maybe we could meet up on a trail. I have to get this woman down this mountain, or I'd stay up here with you. I brought her up, and I have to bring her down."

No fear accompanied the request. I felt so comfortable around him. "Oh, I thought you two were together."

"No, I was just her guide."

"Oh, do you work for a company?" I asked, ready to pay him any amount to help ME down.

"No, I work for God. Today my work was here. She was afraid but wanted to come up. I helped her, and now I'll help her down to her husband."

"Do you mind if I join you?" I asked, ready to follow them anyway.

"Not at all, then maybe we could go get lunch?" he asked.

"Definitely," I said, returning with him to the woman.

"You're not staying up here for the view?" She asked, puzzled. "Don't you want to go the rest of the way? There's another trail that way, and it's breathtaking!"

"I didn't come up here for the view. I came up here for the two of you," I answered confidently. "I had no desire to conquer this trail. I understand now. Take one step at a time . . . such is life. I could stay and look at the view, but I'd rather live in the moment and seize this opportunity. Besides that," I giggled, "I might have to have a plane come and rescue me because I'm not going down this mountain myself!"

The woman smiled and nodded in approval. The man nodded toward the steep rocks. "Remember, we take one step at a time, and you never look at the destination but only your next step. There's no hurry. There's no path. You take the way that looks easiest to you. It doesn't have to be the way I take."

I nodded, knowing his words referred to much more than the red rock in front of us!

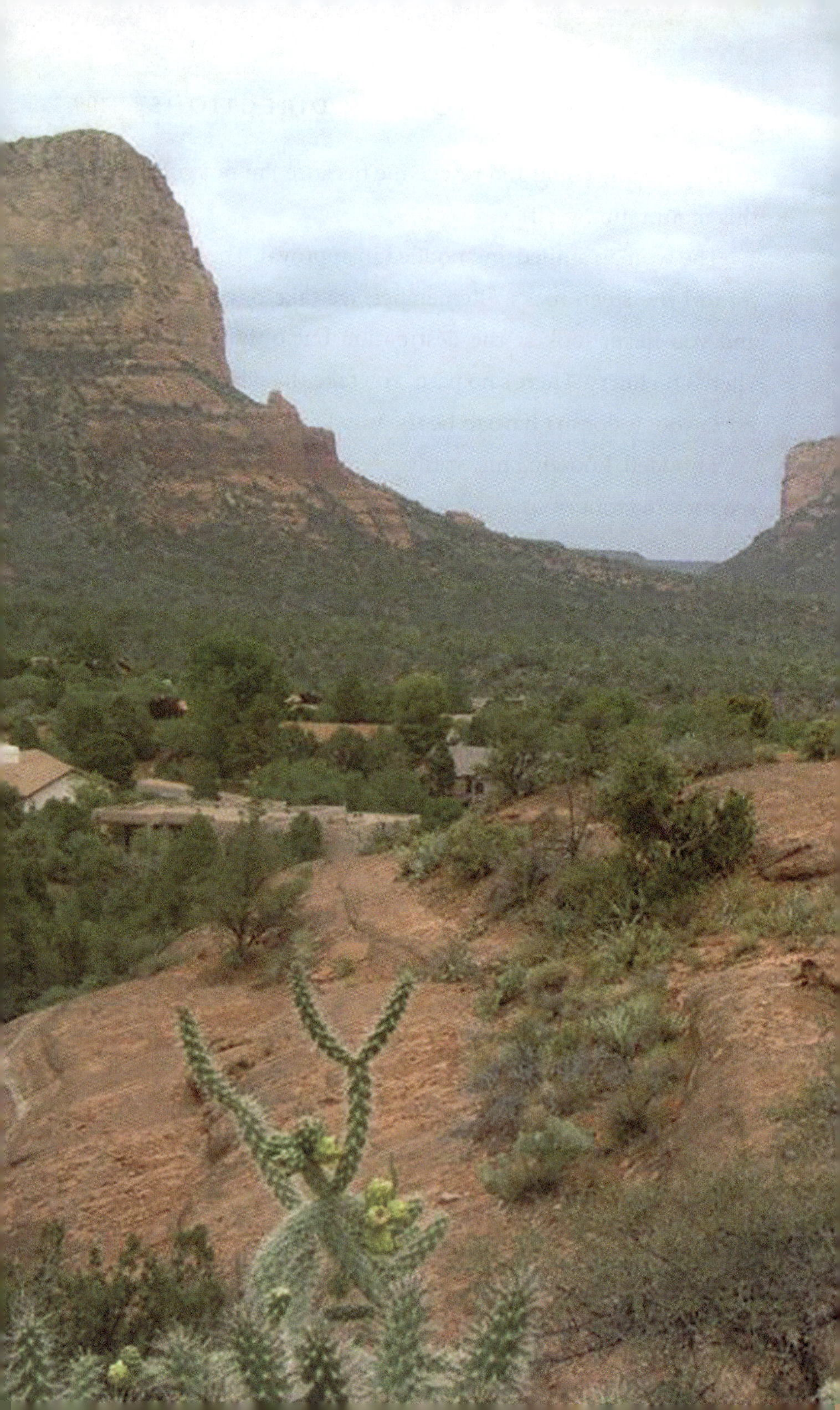

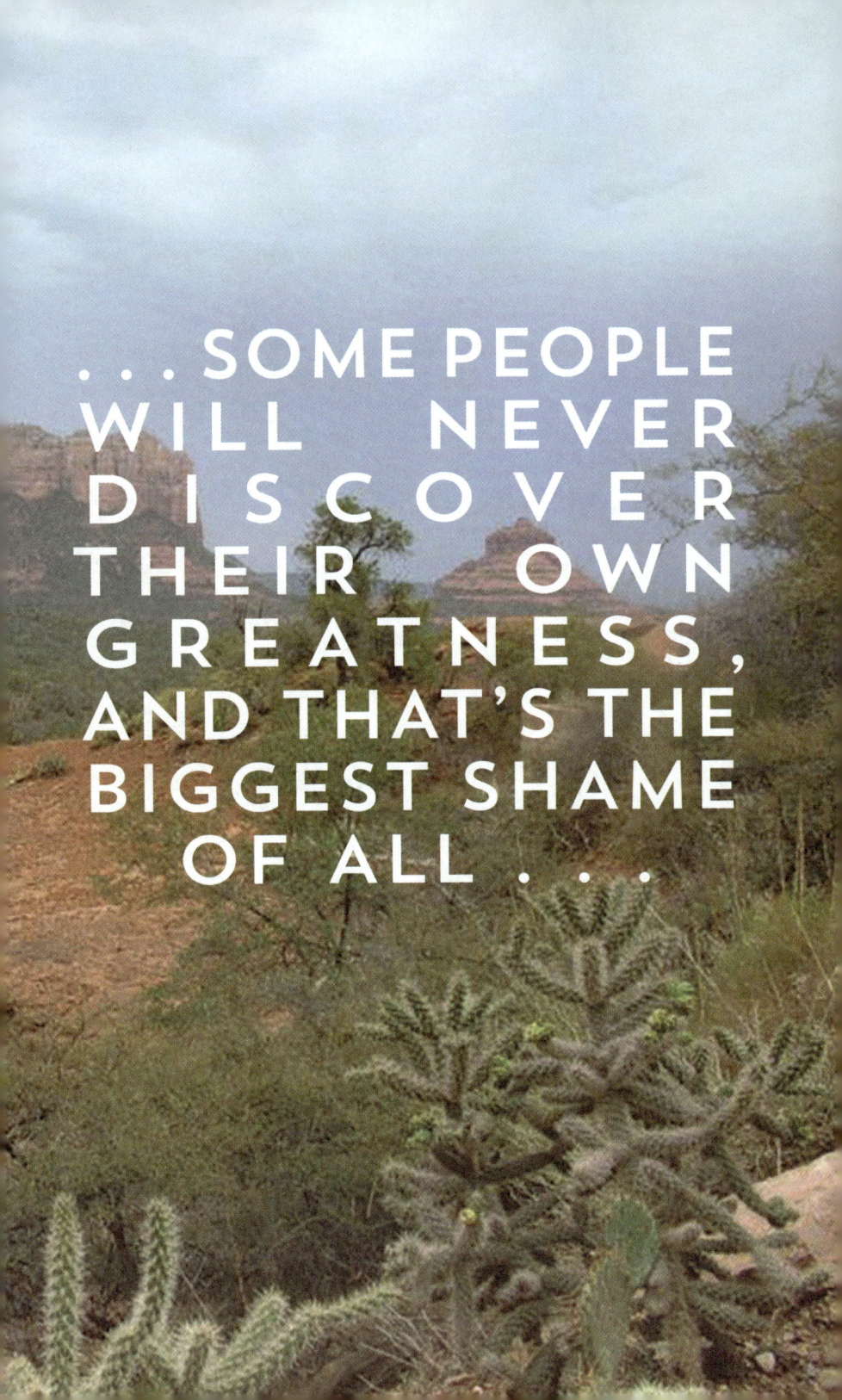

. . . SOME PEOPLE WILL NEVER DISCOVER THEIR OWN GREATNESS, AND THAT'S THE BIGGEST SHAME OF ALL . . .

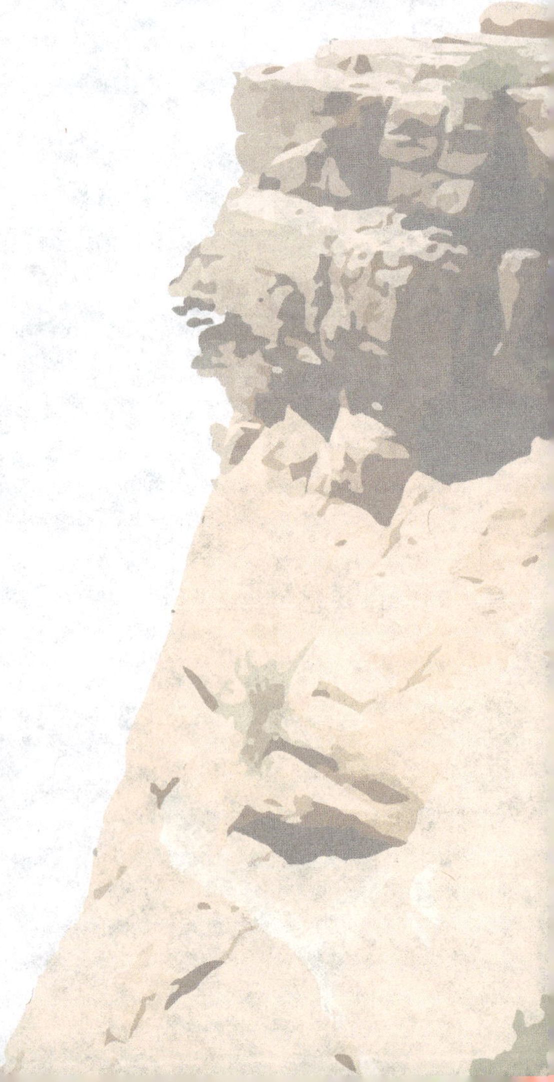

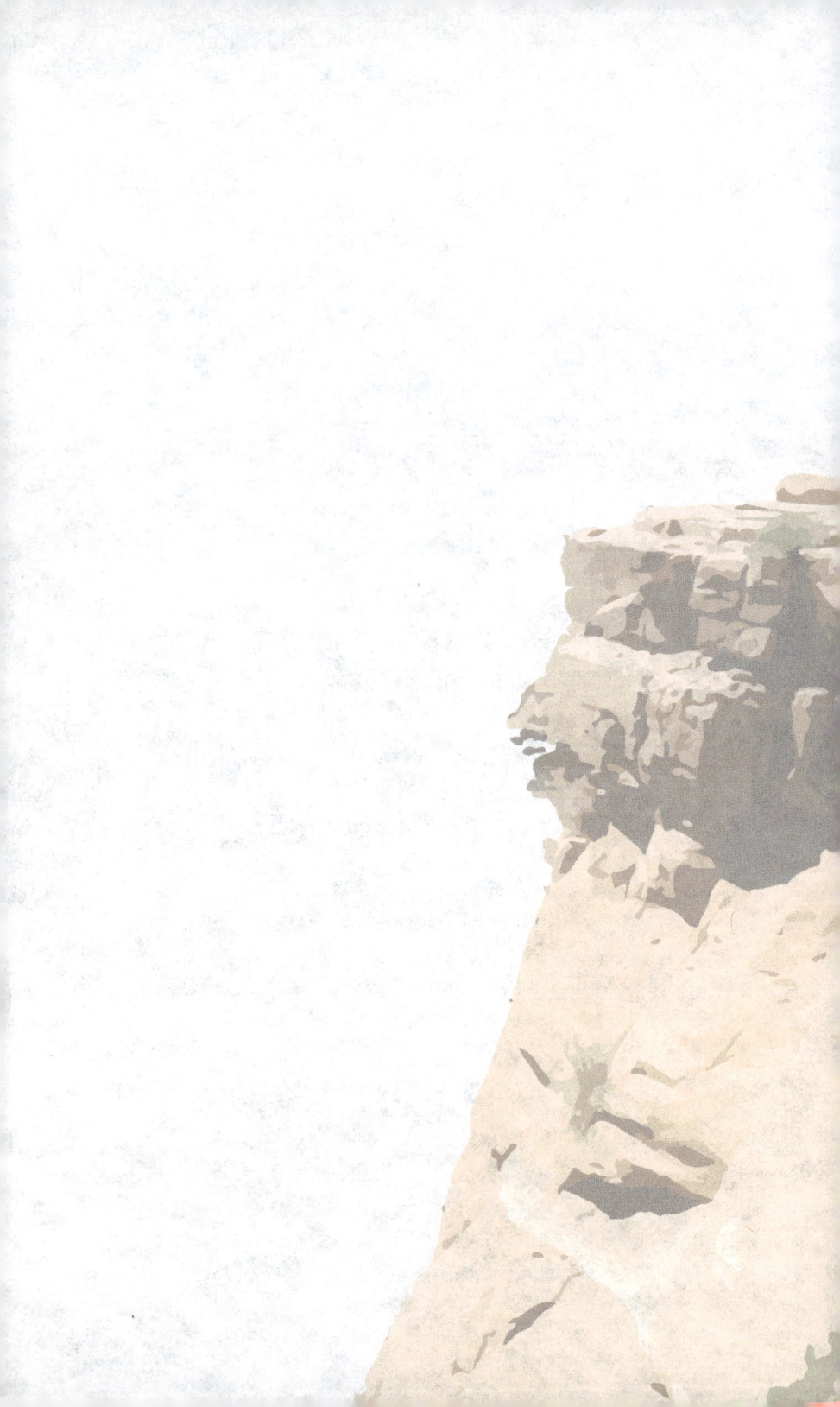

CHAPTER 5

EXPECTATIONS OF THE FUTURE

Immediately Jesus reached out his hand and caught him. "You of little faith," he said, "why did you doubt?"

~ Matthew 14:31

Disappointment comes from expectations. Most people have a plan for their life and a general idea of where they want their life to go. Maybe the plan is to have no plan. Some people plan to follow the normal milestones: go to college, get a job, get married, have children, have grandchildren, retire, travel, die wealthy. Most of society focuses around this ideal, and we are all put together and asked to complete the same academic work in school. We have core classes we are expected to take and do well in. Extracurricular activities are set up if there is enough funding to support them. Some people choose recreational fun, others, music or writing, and some express themselves through art. Many know their interests from a young age. Sometimes these talents are suppressed because society looks down on them. Art is for females, physical activity is for males, and writing is for the "nerds." When our dreams are possibly our purpose, our hearts are never satisfied if we do not achieve those dreams or goals.

Why do some of us feel the need to be like everyone else? Expectations are the enemy. The problem with expecting anything is that we do not control anything but our own actions; therefore, our expectations are completely out of our hands. I am not suggesting that we shouldn't rely on people or should forego having plans; I'm merely telling you that people should not *expect* anything. What's wrong with not knowing what tomorrow brings? When we do not complete things by the timeline we give ourselves, we find disappointment because we *expected* our lives to be in a place where we are not.

Do not confuse goals with expectations. Goals are something we strive for, and they help lead our life in the direction we desire to go. If you go to college and complete the work, you will get a degree. It's something that's attainable because you control it. Pregnancy, marriage, finances, careers, death, etc.—they are things that are beyond any human's complete control. Of course, you can set a goal to assist you with finding these things: eat healthy, live longer; invest in the right stock, gain money; go to college, find a better paying job; have sex at the correct time, get pregnant. Easy, right?

After experiencing life for a number of years, you'll find disappointment at some point in your life. People are in charge of financial companies, people hire people to work, the doctors and surgeons are human, people produce food that can easily become contaminated with the things that people put in the environment, people affect the stock market, people's lifestyles may affect the chances of having a baby, and people take risks that result in death. People are not predictable, because everyone has the potential to change, and each person makes up their own mind on every situation. They can be influenced, persuaded, and driven to make a decision based on their surroundings—with the potential to lead to disappointment. Gratification comes from inside. To find true happiness, you must first search within your own heart and have a solid foundation in faith. We are a small part of the big picture.

We expect teachers to have answers, priests to be holy, firemen to be heroes, lawyers to win, secretaries to answer, students to study, and waiters to be available. They should—it's their job! They are also human and have not reached perfection. This is not a fair assumption, though. We are all sinners and make decisions that could be filed under the "try again" section. The real mistake of it is not trying again. Mistakes will be made, detours will have to be taken, and people will ask to be forgiven. Life does not always have the happy ending, it's not always fair or equal, and things happen that will put patience to the test.

Perhaps as a child, nobody expected anything out of you. Maybe you didn't even expect anything out of yourself. It is harder for some people to pass school, go to college, be involved in the community, or find a job. This isn't always due to work ethic but can be because of socio-economic status. However, we are all equal as far as having the opportunity to go to school, apply for college, apply for a job, and find resources within the community. Maybe it was in your plan to go down the path not as well traveled. Perhaps by taking the rough road in the beginning, God taught you skills that nobody else had and that made a positive impact on the world. There are more areas of the world that need help than are prospering, yet there are millions of people in the world watching it happen rather than fighting against hunger, abuse, or medical issues.

We expect our government to fix problems, our church to reach out to the community, and our schools to educate the rising generation so people don't end up on the street. It's not enough, clearly. Instead of looking at another route or realizing the real fault is lack of respect for each other, we tell the government, "You're spending too much money here! Focus the money on this area." We donate a few dollars to the church and say, "I donate; therefore, I help." We demand that teachers take more tests and kids reach higher standards. It must be the teachers' fault if the children aren't learning. These three organizations impact the statistics on poverty, but if people just helped each other, there wouldn't be as many people dying, suffering, or homeless. I'm not saying, "give, give, give"; I'm writing to "help, help, help." Be the teacher, be the community member who creates jobs, be the person who builds a nonprofit organization, or start fighting for programs you'd like to see the government fund. Sitting back and letting it happen while complaining to your neighbor will never change anything.

Instead of hoping something happens in the future, focus on here and now. If you are constantly looking back, you *will* eventually stumble. If your mind is focused on what happened yesterday or what will happen tomorrow, it cannot register today. You will miss amazing opportunities and sights that God has given you *today*. Today is a new day; embrace it because God made it unique to you. Your day will never be the same as another person's, even if you're together the whole day. Words mean different things to you, and your thoughts are different from your companion's.

The world would be quite amazing if every person reached their full potential—if every single person utilized their unique quality in the world. Some people will never discover their own greatness, and that's the biggest shame of all. You were put on earth to offer something. We were all born to be leaders in some way. God has a plan for you, and if you're not living with His guidance, you will never discover that plan. He gave you a talent, to lead, to write, to dream, to motivate, to help, to cure, to build, or perhaps something completely different from what I've mentioned. You have a talent and it's exactly what you are supposed to do in this world. You may ignore it because, financially, there are better choices. Perhaps you don't follow your dream because someone told you that it's a bad idea. Maybe you're not doing it because there's just no time in your busy day. Whatever the reasons, the desire will never disappear. That little ball of fire within you will continue to burn until you let it go! God gave you that talent, those feelings, and He wants you to use them. Imagine a world where each person was in a career and doing what they loved to do! Imagine the "good" that would appear in the world if we all just focused on what would make "us" happy.

Our decisions affect the world, positively or negatively. Choose positive! Choose good! Choose God's plan and the talent He provided you!

When we follow God's plan, the rest of those earthly things fall into place. He will provide as much money as you need and give you strength when necessary. God always provides but not always in the way we define the word. Plunging into the unknown—whether that's a new relationship, career, or location—is scary. Most humans like staying in the "comfort zone," where we can easily predict most of the day. We like stability. It's hard to trust something we can't prove or see, hear, or touch. Faith is an incredibly hard concept to even understand. It's about believing, but our minds are weak and always ready for the "but what if" scenarios.

Put your trust, your faith, in God. John 14:1 reads, "Do not let your hearts be troubled. You believe in God, believe also in me."

Luke 12:22–23 reads, "Then Jesus said to His disciples: 'Therefore I tell you, do not worry about your life, what you will eat; or about your body, what you will wear. For life is more than food, and the body more than clothes.'" He goes on in verses 31–34 by saying, "But seek His kingdom, and these things will be given to you as well. Do not be afraid, little flock, for your Father has been pleased to give you the kingdom. Sell your possessions and give to the poor. Provide purses for yourselves that will not wear out, a treasure in heaven that will never fail, where no thief comes near and no moth destroys. For where your treasure is, there your heart will be also."

Let the Bible lead your life and trust only in it. Search the Bible for the answers to your most difficult questions. Pray to God each day and ask for His guidance. Trust that Jesus will be back one day and we will all be judged. How much more important is your Creator and Savior than the earthly things that will eventually turn to dust? Believe that with God's grace you can make a difference in any aspect of the world. In fact, we were born to change the world! Also believe that if you do not make that difference, then nothing different will happen. Be the change you hope to see in the world.

PART III, DAY 3, SATURDAY, AUGUST 25: CONSUMING KNOWLEDGE

The man from Cathedral Rock and I met at Mango Café in downtown Sedona for Korean food. It was close to 2:00PM, the weather was warm and beautiful, and we were able to look out at the red rocks during lunch from a small balcony inside the restaurant.

I immediately felt at ease with him. He was an older gentleman, my guess would be in his 60s, and he displayed a very gentle personality that would make the most anxious person relax. His knowledge seemed to radiate from him. He was different from anyone I had ever met. His presence screamed that he had a secret ... an answer ... a wisdom about life.

"What created the energy of confusion with the problem you're facing?" he asked.

"Fear," I answered matter-of-factly. "With every question, it's fear. I let past experiences control the present."

"Go back into life and what created the belief. Release it to God."

"Give my problems to God?"

"Yes, ask Him to take the problems but give you the wisdom of them. Ask God to help you realize all the experiences from the past. Often when you ask for the wisdom of why you have these problems, you find that it was their truth, not your own."

I squinted at him, trying to understand his meaning. "You mean the truth of the person who created it?"

"Whatever you see and experience in life, you make the decision to keep that energy. For example, if your eyes are drawn to a fight. Often you are focusing on your own anger. Everything you make a judgment on is yours. You own it. It's your mirror. The greatest way to be of service to this planet is to clear your own emotions and fears into divine perfection!"

I took a small sip of my hot green tea and thought about his words. "You're saying that some people will not give a fight a second thought because they don't own anger. Other people will watch the fight or feel the effects of it because they have anger within them?"

"Yes."

"How do I get rid of it?"

"Just give it to God. It's that easy," he answered, pausing as the waitress put our lunch in front of us. "Do you mind if I say a small prayer to thank God for this food?"

I shook my head. I wasn't used to praying before a meal, but I wasn't uncomfortable.

As he finished, he picked back up with his sentence. "Giving it to God is as simple as saying, 'God, release my anger. Help me understand the wisdom of why I have it, but take the feeling.' Do that with everything negative in your life: guilt, sadness, hate, anger, frustration, irritation, etc. When you think about it, throw it away. Your mind will try to think of it, but keep asking God to help you understand why you're thinking of it and work in your life to resolve those problems and forgive the events or people that caused them."

"I get it," I answered. A bright light seemed to shine down on my heart as every situation I'd ever encountered in life seemed to flash through my mind. For the next several minutes, I could see a countless number of small lines being drawn in my mind. Everything was making sense! All my problems seemed to slowly dissolve in my mind, crumbling before my eyes. "I'm in the exact place I'm supposed to be at exactly the time I should be," I thought. This man had just given me wisdom I'd use for the rest of my life!

We spent the day together on that beautiful Saturday. I felt so much peace from talking to the man whom I may never see again. The truth is that I don't need to see him again. I hope we do meet again one day, but I'm content with the everlasting impact he made on my life that day. God put him on that path because I made an agenda. God timed it perfectly. He knew I was ready to receive the information the man was about to give. People helping people; it's exactly what the world is about.

The sun eventually went down, leaving the red rocks nothing but a dark formation in the distance. We sat on a wooden bench in downtown, letting a warm breeze brush lightly over us. Faint lights from the streetlights of the main street illuminated the area, giving the town a warm feel.

"Why don't you write?" I asked him after a long silence. "You could have a best seller."

He smiled at me and touched my shoulder. "That's your job. I teach through talking. You will teach through writing. We are all born with a unique talent. This is mine, and that," he nodded toward the notepads in my hiking bag, "is yours. We all make the decision to utilize our talent. Don't let yours go to waste."

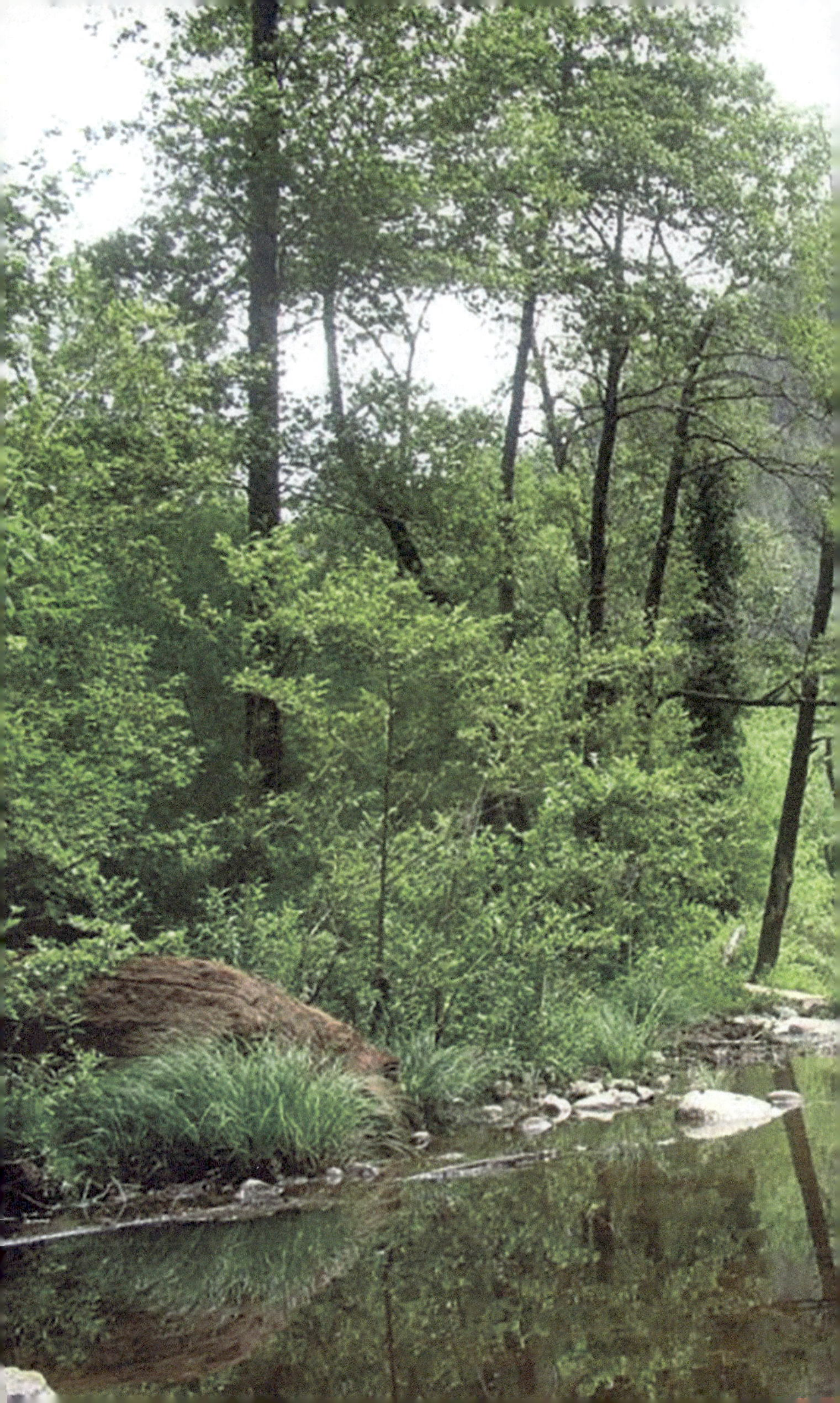

. . . COINCIDENCE? I DON'T BELIEVE THERE IS SUCH A THING. PURPOSE? ALWAYS!

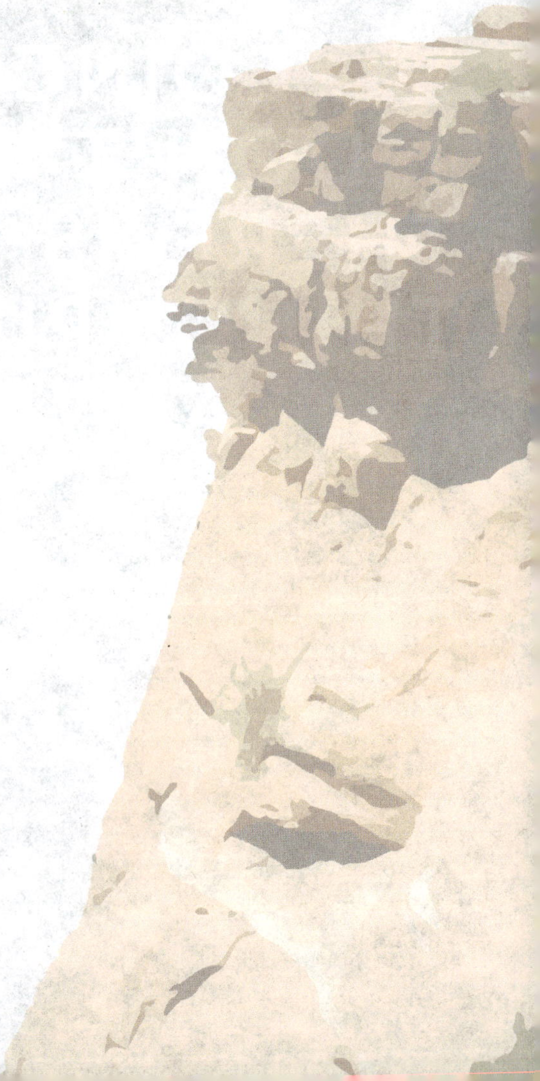

CHAPTER 6

THE RACE TO JUDGMENT

Who is wise and understanding among you? Let them show it by their good life, by deeds done in the humility that comes from wisdom. But if you harbor bitter envy and selfish ambition in your hearts, do not boast about it or deny the truth. Such "wisdom" does not come down from heaven but is earthly, unspiritual, demonic. For where you have any envy and selfish ambition, there you find disorder and every evil practice.

~ James 3:13–16

Coincidence? I don't believe there is such a thing. Purpose? Always! God controls timing, and I believe people are entered into your life at exactly the time God meant for them to be there. Each person is supposed to teach the other person something. Some people are meant to stay, while others are merely bridges to get you to the other side of your path. Everyone needs help on his or her journey through life. Everyone!

God put us on this earth with billions of other people. He didn't do that for you to be individualized in everything you do. God wants you to talk to people, interact with them, and share your knowledge. Why would God give you so much knowledge, experiences, and a unique gift if you were supposed to keep it to yourself? He's so creative, and He designed an environment where *we* can also be creative.

By having Jesus in your life, you are doing His work—for Him—through yourself. You are putting Him first and yourself second. Personally, I feel that faith is such a hard thing to understand for someone who has not studied the Bible. Faith is *more* than believing in God . . . you are accepting that God is in control. By having faith, you believe God is most powerful and has the ability to change anything about your life. You believe He can make miracles happen. Faith is believing in God when everything in life tells you He's not there and He's not interested.

Every person in the Bible had a hardship. They didn't lose faith; they just questioned it. Before Sarah became pregnant with Abraham's baby at an old age, she laughed at the thought. How was God going to give her a child when she was past childbearing age? That's why her son, Isaac, was named after the Hebrew word for "laughter." Never doubt God's power! He created the world; how can He not fix your problem? Our problems are not as big as the world, although in our minds we tend to believe that. The story of Jesus is amazing! From the Immaculate Conception, to Him willingly going to the cross to die for people who despised Him. If you are a Christian, then you believe the entire story. If you believe the entire story, then you know it's beyond our ability

THE RACE TO JUDGMENT 129

to comprehend. Imagine His story happening today... would you be one who followed Him? Would you shout degrading things to Him? Would you be the one who tries to give Him water as He walks by? Would you have remained silent in fear that the officials would bring retaliation on you? What kind of Christian are you? There's only one real kind.

Society is full of judgment by Christians and non-Christians alike. If we each spent more time encouraging rather than judging, I'm convinced that people would be happier and more productive. While forming an opinion is natural, we should refrain from believing any person is "better" than another. One sin does not outweigh another. All sin is equal, and we all do it. The most common opinions I hear regarding church and religion include the following:

"I grew up going to church every Sunday. I need a break from it."

"Why would I want to be a part of religion? THOSE people go to church, and when they exit the door, they are the ones who are drinking, stealing, and being rude to other people."

"Church is boring."

"You want me to go to church when there are priests molesting little boys? Why would I follow any word from a person like that?"

"I'm a Christian, but I don't have to read the Bible or go to church to know Jesus."

"Church is full of hypocrites."

"I'm too busy for church. I go on the important days like Christmas and Easter."

"I'm a good person. I'll go to heaven even if I don't go to church."

"My kids are bored in church."

"It's too early on a Sunday. I should be able to sleep in—it's the weekend!"

"How can there be so many religions? How do you even know who to believe?"

"The church just wants money."

Religion and spirituality is an individual experience. Although one person gives a sermon and everyone hears the same information, every person processes the information differently. There is only one Bible; however, we have multiple religions because people interpret word meanings and sentences in different ways. Many people go to church to seek a relationship with God, while others go because it is routine or a social experience. Why are church and religion important? When Jesus walked the earth, He spent a lot of time praying. He taught the Word of God and listened to it. If the Son of God was listening and preaching the Lord's Word, how much more important is it for us? Although Jesus knew what the future held for Him, he also knew the importance of fulfilling God's plan even if it caused Him pain. How easy it would have been for Jesus to become arrogant as people fell to their knees, thanking Him for healing them. It would also have been easy for Him to save Himself and stop his persecutors from pursuing Him, but it wasn't in the plan. Jesus came to show us how to live. We should know how Jesus dealt with judgment and act the same.

People are people and they are full of flaws, which means they won't always make the godly choice. Reflect on yourself. You follow God, but you don't do everything correctly. Nobody deserves the kingdom of heaven, because we all sin. We all have judged and have done things that we know are not the best choice(s). Pastors and priests are people too, and sometimes they make mistakes. Being a servant of the Lord does not mean that you enter into a bubble that nobody can pop. Sure, you can create a bubble, but someone will always try to pop it. The world has evil within it, and sometimes temptation creates choices that are not in our best interest. Maybe we unknowingly choose it, or maybe we have a really weak moment and don't care. Either way, we will stumble on our journey. If we continue to believe that people who make mistakes shouldn't be in religious roles, then we wouldn't have any religious leaders. Nobody is perfect, including me. Aside from that, it is not our place to judge right from wrong. In His perfect timing, God will.

Judgment. Name calling, aggression, deceit, abuse, disrespect, degrading remarks, theft, murder . . . with so much wrongdoing, how can a person refrain from judging another's actions? How can you forgive a person who abused you or murdered your family member? Hmm . . . this might be the single most important thing God has taught us: forgiveness. Jesus suffered as He was flogged, ridiculed, beaten, and eventually crucified. Imagine large nails being hammered through your wrists and ankles! Imagine thorns poking into your head as you're stripped naked and ridiculed. Imagine being flogged while your hands are tied and people shout degrading remarks to you. Imagine being spit on, laughed at, and called a liar. Jesus had the ability to destroy those who did all that to Him and prove Himself. He didn't. Instead, He asked God to forgive them!

Many times we believe a bad situation is the result of a wrong choice, but as times goes on, we realize how it helped us. Sometimes it really was a "bad" situation, but other times it simply only appeared to be terrible. Faith is patience. To fully understand why you're going through the negative things in life, you must have faith and patience. Parts of life will always surpass understanding. However, believe that HE is going to take you where you need to go. By letting God direct your life and accepting His support and encouragement, you will surely find the peace that awaits you. Give Him praise, because without Him, you would have never made it as far as you have. He will guide you as long as you allow Him.

When you are negative, it's because you choose to let negativity control your life. If you have problems with love, it's because you've chosen to let that affect you. Believe that God has a plan for you! Ask Him to guide you to the one you are supposed to be with. If you are having trouble paying bills, perhaps it's because you made the decisions that ultimately put you in the place you are today. Perhaps you are in the situation because of another person's decisions. Either way, God can make every situation, good or bad, lead back to the path He has planned for you. Not every bad situation will be the result of bad decisions. Sometimes those "bad" decisions turn out to be the best decisions of our lives. It doesn't mean they were bad decisions; it doesn't mean they were good decisions. They were just decisions. Take everything at face value. Your decision, every single decision, has put you in the place you are today! We can either thank God for good will or wish that we never had to deal with it. You can either dance in the rain, curse it because it ruined your plans, or admire it from indoors. You can write the book, read the book, or hear about the book. You can be the person who makes a difference or the person who pretends to make a difference.

You are only as good as you act when nobody is watching. That's the person you are. Would you donate money if you didn't get credit or couldn't write it off on taxes? Would you volunteer if your name never were mentioned? Would you lie or steal if you wouldn't get caught? Would you cheat if your significant other gave you permission? Would you say sorry if the person weren't repentant? Would you buy items from someone who was using the money to buy drugs or support trafficking? Would you sell porn if it were guaranteed to bring in thousands of dollars a week? Would you say you don't believe in God to save your life at gunpoint? How is your character defined?

Matthew 7:1-5 reads, "Do not judge, or you too you will be judged. For in the same way you judge others, you will be judged, and with the measure you use, it will be measured to you. Why do you look at the speck of sawdust in your brother's eye and pay no attention to the plank in your own eye? How can you say to your brother, 'Let me take the speck out of your eye,' when all the time there is a plank in your own eye? You hypocrite, first take the plank out of your own eye, and then you will see clearly to remove the speck from your brother's eye."

If we are always keeping God as a priority and loving everyone as our neighbor, then the answers to the questions above wouldn't require any thought at all. He tells us that whatever we want others to do for us, we should do the same for them. If people could obey this one command, this one instruction, the world would be good. There would be peace. By putting other people ahead of yourself, you are improving your own life. God will reward this behavior by taking your life and putting it in places you never imagined it could go.

Choices are made every single day, every second. Your choices affect the lives of other people because those decisions create opportunities that another person takes advantage of. God let us do it! He's a part of it every step of the way. We wouldn't even have the ability to think without Him, let alone make an impact. Nothing is a coincidence, but it's all part of a bigger plan that we will never fully understand. When someone needs help, we should provide assistance. When someone is hungry, we should feed them, and when someone is lost, we need to help them find their destination. We are all teachers of Christ. His Spirit should radiate out from each of us so that people can see Him working through us.

THURSDAY, AUGUST 23: AIRPORT EXAMINATION

At the airport on my way to Sedona, I was behind an older woman traveling alone who was clearly from another country.

She spoke very little English and was moving slowly because of having two oversized bags and a cane. Her silver hair and arthritic body led me to believe she was in her 80s, maybe 90s. I watched her slowly make her way to the security gate. Close by, an official was announcing that shoes had to come off, all liquids had to be put in a separate bag, and everything had to be in a bin. A long, impatient line had formed behind this woman, who continued to be oblivious to anyone in a hurry. Her short arms struggled to lift a bag up on the edge of the conveyer belt before she started to take everything out of it and put the items in separate bins (shoes in one, coat in another, belt in another, and so on). She lifted a book bag up on the belt which was clearly too wide for the belt. She tried to fit the large bag inside the provided plastic bin, no doubt thinking she was following the instructions of the security guard. It immediately toppled over, hitting her five bins of separated items and sending them all falling to the ground. She was in the process of taking off her shoes and now had everything to clean up. I looked over at security, who stood watching her pick up all the items. I could hear people sighing in annoyance. I waited a few seconds before I removed myself from the line and went over to assist the elderly woman.

"Hi," I said, picking up a bag from the floor.

She looked at me with no response. No English.

I motioned to her bag and pointed to the conveyer belt, instructing her that she didn't have to put the bag in the small bin. I also pointed to her shoes and belt and wallet and coat. "These can all go together." I made the motions by pointing and showing her they could fit in just one bin rather than five different ones.

Her watery eyes were sincere as she nodded gratefully. I smiled at her and grabbed two bins—all she would need. Security immediately came over and instructed me to go back in line.

"She needed help," I responded as I returned to my original place in line.

I returned to my place. The lady in front of me smiled. "I'm glad you did that. I was wondering why nobody was helping her!"

I politely nodded. "We all make the choice," I said, watching security finally help the lady successfully navigate through the line.

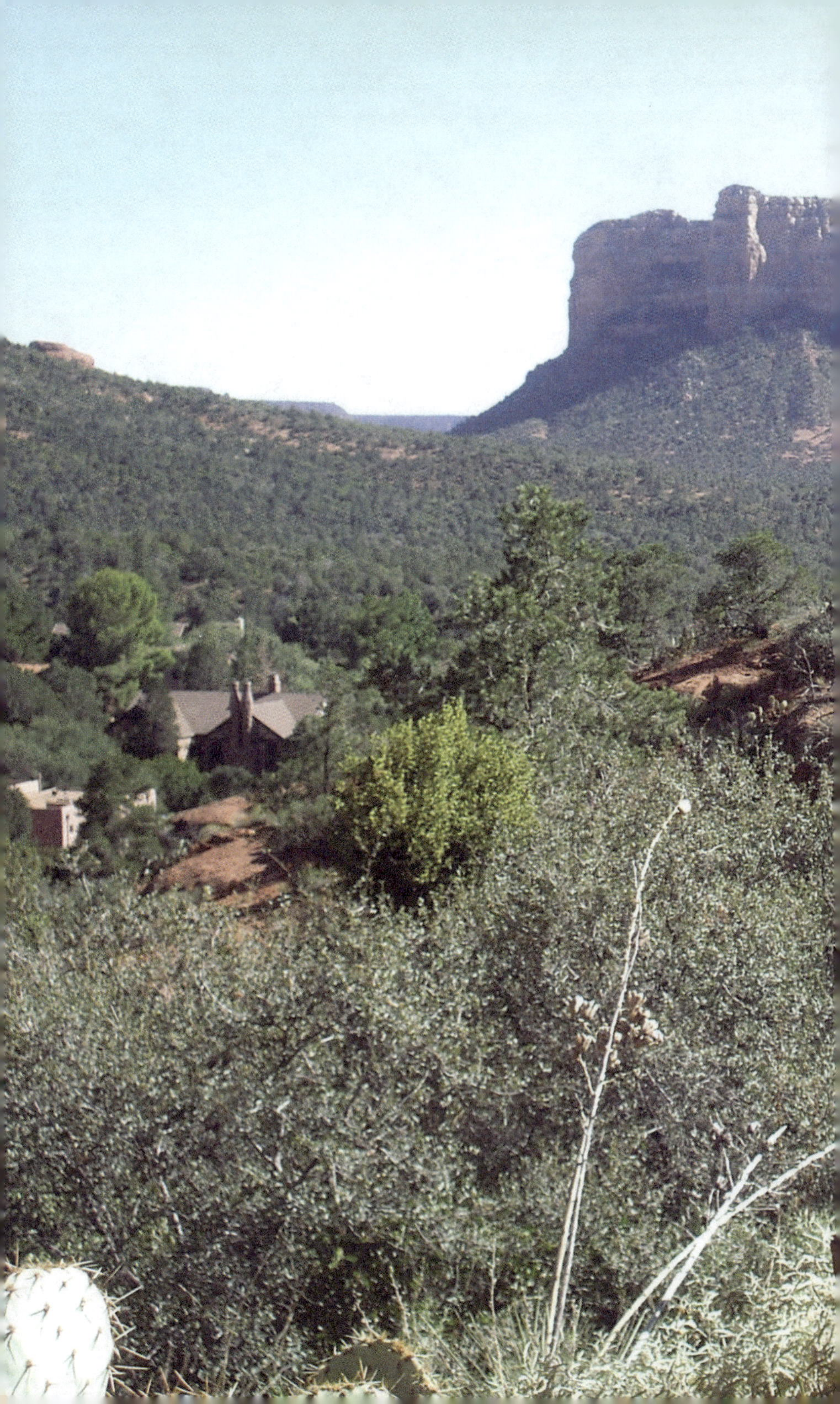

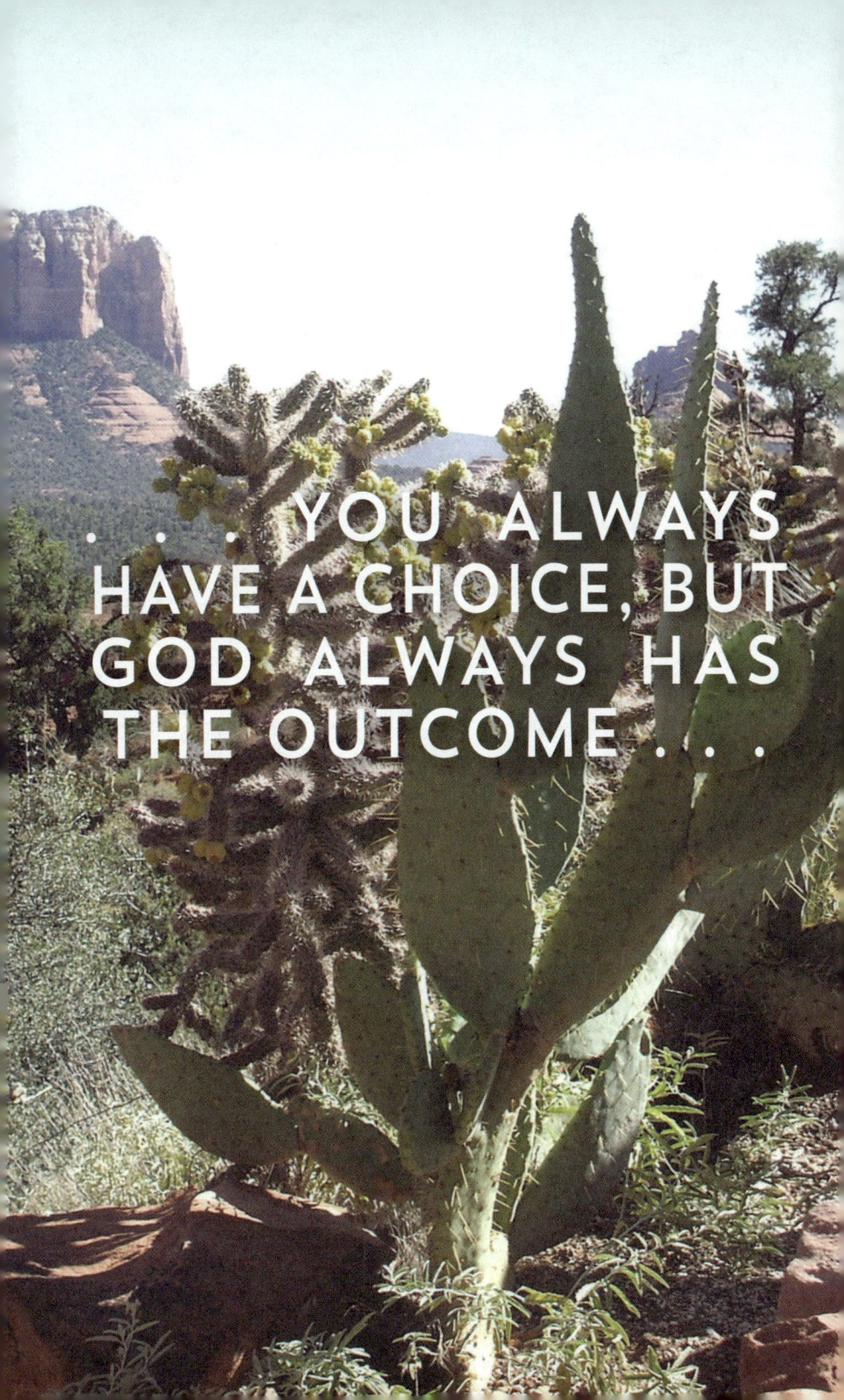

. . . YOU ALWAYS HAVE A CHOICE, BUT GOD ALWAYS HAS THE OUTCOME . . .

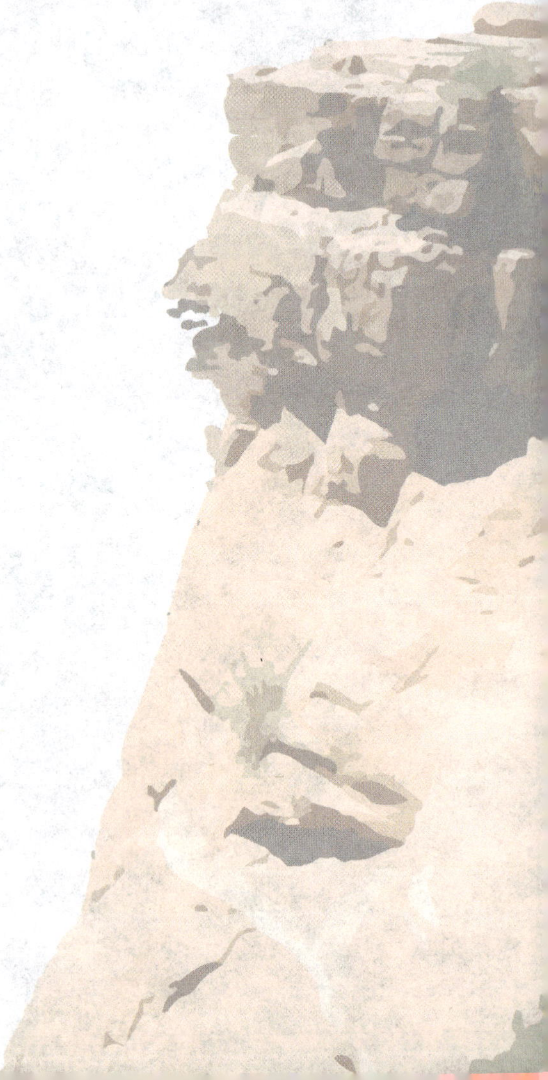

CHAPTER 7

REACHING THE TOP

He heals the brokenhearted and binds up their wounds.

~ Psalm 147:3

God will heal the brokenhearted and put His arms around each of His children to comfort them. We are God's children if we choose to be. There's nothing we can do that God will not forgive if we repent. There's not a person on this earth who is destined for hell if he or she makes the decision to trust in God and follow Him. We receive God's love because we were born His children. We were born with a purpose, the ability to love, and the power to change the world. It's only because we deny Him that the devil has any power over us.

On hearing this, Jesus said, "It is not the healthy who need a doctor, but the sick. But go and learn what this means: 'I desire mercy, not sacrifice.' For I have not come to call the righteous, but sinners."

~ Matthew 9:12–13

In a world filled with hatred, there is one thing that we can look forward to and find comfort within: salvation. God doesn't hate you for anything you've done but rather loves you so much He decided to send His ONLY Son to bear pain and suffering and ultimately die for each and every one of us. Jesus hung on the cross for you, for me, and for them. He could have removed Himself from it. After all, the people He was dying for were the people executing Him. What if the world functioned like that today? What if we treated everyone the way Jesus treated His persecutors?

> On one occasion an expert in the law stood up to test Jesus. "Teacher," he asked, "what must I do to inherit eternal life?"
>
> "What is written in the Law?" he replied, "How do you read it."
>
> He answered: "Love the Lord your God with all your heart and with all your soul and with all your strength and with all your mind, and love your neighbor as yourself."
>
> "You have answered correctly," Jesus replied, "Do this, and you will live."
>
> ~ Luke 10:25–28

Living without God or Jesus is similar to trying to dig a hole under water. Have you ever dug a hole beneath the water in a lake? Dig, water goes in it, and sand caves into the hole. Dig again and the same thing happens. It's routine and boring, not to mention meaningless. Even if you succeed, you can do nothing with a hole beneath the water because we weren't born to stay under water. It's worth it if you find something as you dig though, right? If it's valuable, sure! Dig deep enough in life, and you will find the most valuable thing on this earth—salvation. It's so valuable there is no price, and the more people who have it, a better place the world would be.

Jesus is a gift that cannot be taken away. He's not a gift that goes bad or out of style or doesn't fit. He's a gift that belongs to everyone. He's one gift that includes healing, comfort, positivity, energy, love, forgiveness, understanding, grace, mercy, and salvation. His gift was given without the thought that you need to give something back. You just have to accept it. Pray for Him to come over you and be a part of your daily life. Invite Him in with conversation in the morning and at night. Think of Him throughout the day as you make decisions. He will change your life for the better, if you allow it, no matter how many times you think you have failed to impress Him.

Over the time that Jesus walked the earth, people knew He was different. Here was a man who was healing people on the Sabbath day, inviting tax collectors to walk with Him, saving prostitutes, touching those with leprosy and healing them, and challenging those in authority. Jesus didn't fear death; He knew His purpose on earth and pursued it. Jesus' life was memorable. He's the most influential historical figure of all time. Jesus put God's Word as a priority, listened to His instructions, and spent every day pursuing the path that God had for Him. I'm sure there were plenty of other paths that were more appealing to Him than the path that led to flogging, ridiculing, and ultimately a crucifixion. Jesus knew what was going to happen, yet He did not run away from it because He knew it was God's plan. Isn't that how we should live our lives? Following God's plan no matter what the consequence and no matter what path looks more appealing.

No task is too large for our God. There is nothing He cannot handle. He can multitask and do things that humans cannot comprehend because it's impossible to be knowledgeable about skills that we do not and cannot possess. God experienced pain, heartbreak, and anger; He knows how we feel in those moments of being "on the edge." He wants you to bring your problems to Him and leave them. Too often we try to fix our own problems, and that simply cannot be done. Ask God for help with your problems and release them to Him. Don't give Him a time limit or expect a certain outcome. Don't ask for a solution but leave it to Him, completely up to Him. The solution might be within you or another person, or it may appear to go unanswered because we never discover the answer.

Our plan is not always the best plan. God knows best, and He will make sure your life goes in a positive direction EVERY time you ask. When things seem to be going poorly, KNOW that there are great things ahead of you, think positively, and go forward with faith. Immediately dismiss any negativity.

Forgive. Once you ask God to take your problems, then it's time to forgive those who caused them. Forgiveness is eliminating the negativity from your life and refusing to think about it again. It remains in silence because you've personally overcome the negative impact it's made on your life. Not over it yet? Choose to be! Pray to God for help. Read the Bible and learn from the triumphs and failures in it. It's all been written. You're not the first to experience it. The Bible is the single most important book in the world. You will be forgiven the same way you forgive others. If God can forgive us, then we can certainly forgive each other.

Everyone has fallen short of earning a place in heaven. That's why Jesus saved us. We spend our lives continuously falling short of heaven, which is such an amazing gift. What can we ever do to earn it? The good news is God is letting you have it if you receive it! Accept His gift if you haven't already done so; it's waiting. When you fail to live according to God's way, then repent. Learn from your mistakes, be sorry for them, and you will be forgiven. You cannot continuously make the same mistake and be forgiven just because you go to church on Sunday and you say a halfhearted "sorry." You might be standing in front of the pastor, who declares your sins forgiven, but unless you are truly sorry for them, they remain with you. God knows your thoughts and feelings, not just your actions. You cannot outsmart your Creator, and you shouldn't want to. Learn from life!

You always have a choice, but God always has the outcome. Listen to the Holy Spirit as you arrive in places on your path that look like detours. Sometimes it's worth taking the shorter path, but other times it is best to enjoy the longer journey. God has provided a variety of scenery and experiences for you. Embrace them. You will never get back THIS moment. Take life, walk with it, and enjoy every second.

DAY 4, AUGUST 26, 2012: THE FINAL HOURS

Sunday morning I woke up at 6:00 AM, ready to embrace the warm, sunny day in Sedona. As I packed up my room, I knew I was ready to leave. God and I had accomplished all we needed to make me ready to begin my path of self-discovery and peace. I started off the day at the Chapel of the Holy Cross, reading my Bible. I sat on the edge of red rock that overlooked the mountains and houses. Silence rested over the city as I admired the beautiful combination of red and green. I closed my eyes to pray. God's arms wrapped around me like they'd done the first day of my arrival, except this time it wasn't to catch my tears but rather to direct me to the next part of my own trail.

Write.

A feeling came over me, and I knew God was asking me to write. Write about everything I had seen and heard in the last few days, put it together, and help change the world, one life at a time. (I'd spend the next year following those specific directions. This unique vacation did bring some people closer to God, and there's nothing in the world that's better than that.) As I looked at the sky, I was reminded of my skydiving adventure—to take a leap of faith. Put my faith in God with my writing and do what I believe He's always been asking me to do.

Two hours later, I entered Christ Lutheran Church on Chapel Road, where the people were inviting and friendly. I immediately asked about communion and if I could take it since I attended a Lutheran church back home. The people were enthusiastic about getting to know more about me and the reason for my visit. Although I didn't know the name of a single person within the room, I felt companionship. I imagine this is how every person "should" feel inside a church. Perhaps it was my mindset, the people, the beautiful scenery, or maybe just a great sermon.

Outside to the left of me was the path where I had met the man who taught me that rushing through life will cause us to stumble. It's important to take one step at a time and trust our Lord and Savior. He taught me to release my troubles because they're not worth the energy of holding. He taught me that one person can make a difference in the life of another, even within a few hours (or minutes).

After the service, I thanked the pastor for a wonderful sermon and walked out to the parking lot, where an older woman stopped me. "Are you moving here?" she asked.

I smiled sincerely at her because I now knew the answer. The answer was simple. The man with the rock heart taught me that I didn't have to be in Sedona to be with God. What's a vortex? A place with rock. I can be just as close to God sitting on my green grass because God isn't a place. He hears us in our best and worst hour, no matter our location. He taught me that I could find peace in the middle of a loud, crowded room because peace resides within us. He taught me that beauty can be found wherever I look, not just on top of a mountain.

"No, but this is going to be a vacation I take every year."

"We would love for you to return."

"I most definitely will. Even when I'm not physically here, a piece of my heart will always stay," I said, glancing at the cross outside the building. The red rocks seemed to smile in the background of the church as I closed my eyes to take a moment to breathe in the silence, make a mental note of the scenery, and to say thank you to God for answering my every prayer in exactly the way it was meant to be.

I know a secret. God whispered it in the air and sent it down to me. My heart heard it, my hands have written it . . . and now you have read it.

> Finally, be strong in the Lord and in his mighty power. Put on the full armor of God, so that you can take your stand against the devil's schemes. For our struggle is not against flesh and blood, but against the rulers, against the authorities, against the powers of this dark world and against the spiritual forces of evil in the heavenly realms. Therefore put on the full armor of God, so that when the day of evil comes, you may be able to stand your ground, and after you have done everything, to stand.
>
> ~ Ephesians 6:10–13

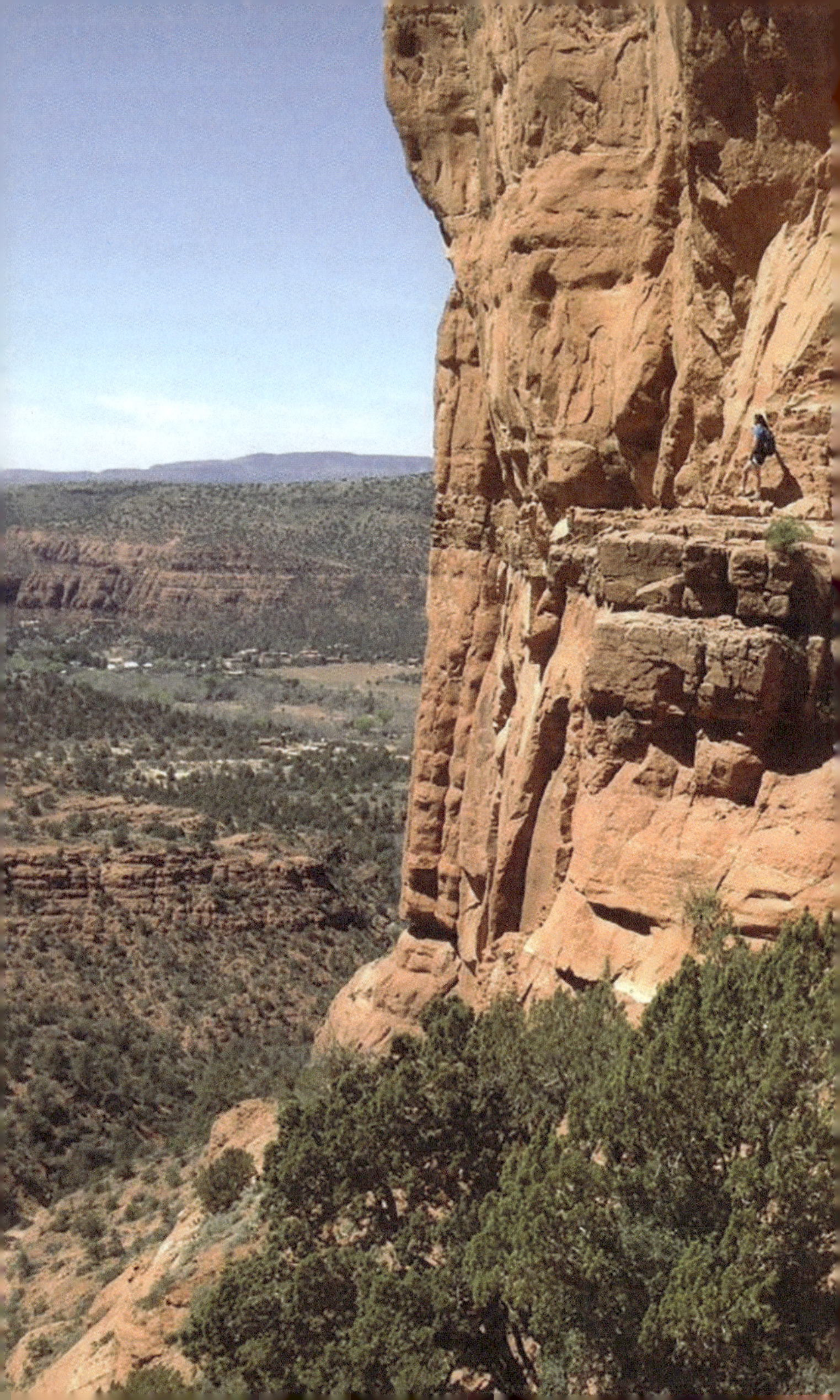

... I KNOW A SECRET. GOD WHISPERED IT IN THE AIR AND SENT IT DOWN TO ME. MY HEART HEARD IT, MY HANDS HAVE WRITTEN IT ... AND NOW YOU HAVE READ IT ...

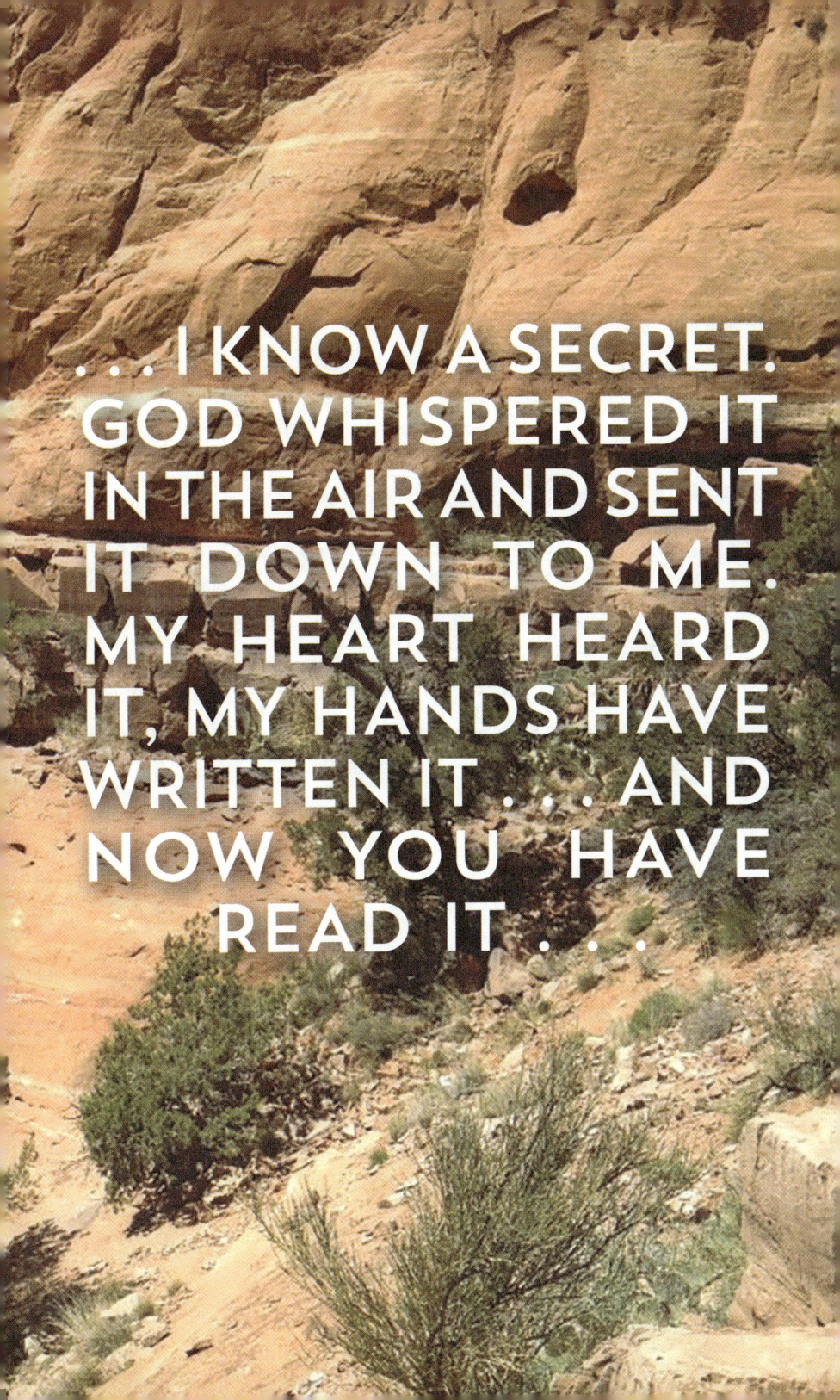

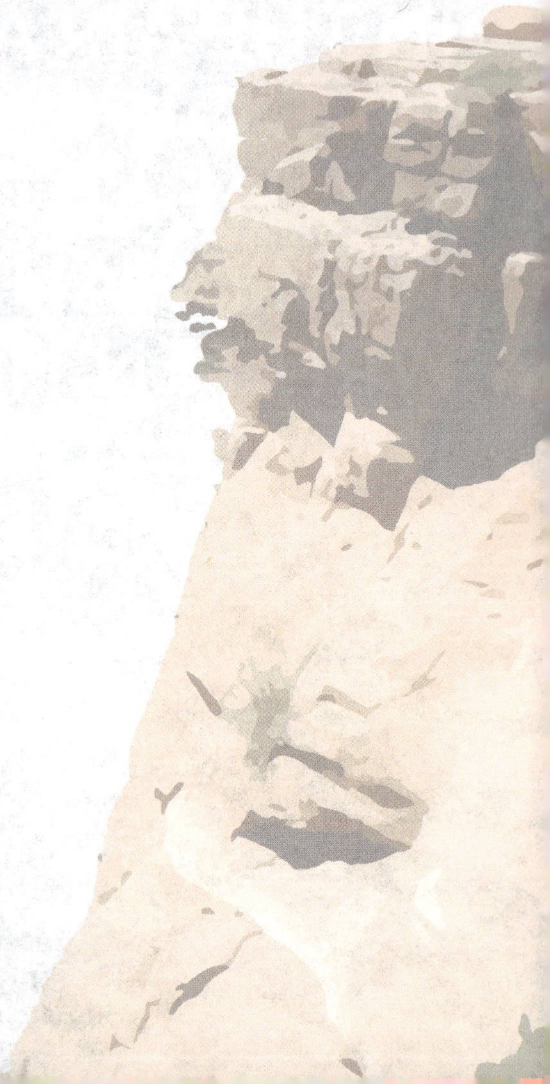

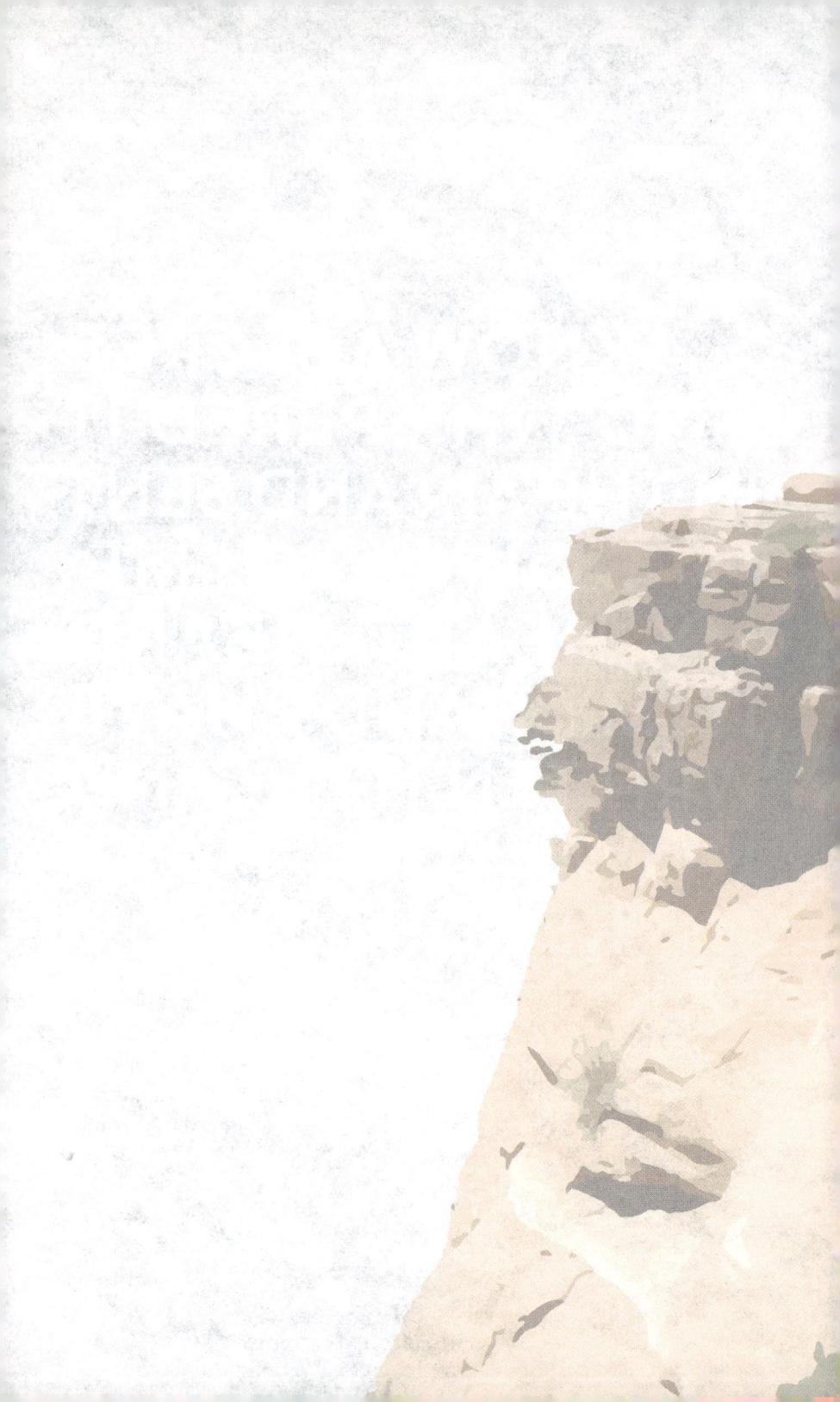

PHOTOGRAPHY INDEX

Page 38: A picture of me by the airport and Sky Ranch Lodge on a small overlook that gives a fantastic view of Sedona.

Page 41: Airport Loop Trail, a 3.25 mile hike that wraps around the airport and gives great views of Sedona. On this trail, God taught me to slow down and trust in Him.

Page 45: God promised in Genesis 9:14–15 that He would never destroy the earth again with water. This promise is solidified through the rainbow. On Friday, August 24, the first day God and I "bonded," a double rainbow could be seen over the red rocks of Sedona.

Page 65: The caterpillar I found while hiking on Boynton Canyon Trail. Soon after, I discovered a butterfly and realized how important and beautiful every breathing thing can be in the world, no matter how slow or little.

Page 68: The man who called me with his beautiful music while sitting on the top of Boynton Canyon Vista. This is the same man that would climb down and hand me a heart made from the red rock.

Page 71: The beautifully carved rock I received from "the flute man" while hiking on Boynton Vista. His words of wisdom will resonate within me for the rest of my life. He taught me that peace is within ourselves and cannot be found in a location.

Page 91: Skydiving at Red Rock Skydiving in Cottonwood, Arizona. We flew over Sedona before jumping out of an airplane 10,000 feet up.

Page 103: As I sat by this tree for multiple hours, I not only developed peace in my mind but also started a daily relationship with God that has only continued to grow stronger every day. I do not attribute this blessing to the tree but rather that this was the first place I gave God my full attention.

Page 104: A picture I took while climbing to the top of Cathedral Rock. I never would have guessed the blessing that God had waiting for me at the top. This is where I learned to never look beyond my next step but instead to focus on the present.

Page 122: Mango Café, a Korean restaurant that once sat in downtown Sedona. This restaurant is no longer in business; however, this is where I enjoyed green tea and took notes from the blue-eyed man who "worked for God."

Cover Photo: A picture of me sitting on the top of Cathedral Rock. The photo was taken by another hiker at the top of Cathedral Rock.

ABOUT THE AUTHOR

Stacie J. Ourlian is currently a middle school special education teacher and coach in Monroe County, Michigan. She earned a bachelor's degree in special education (cognitive impairments), a master's degree in administration, and a license as an EMT.

She served as the director for Special Olympics in Monroe County for more than four years. Stacie has devoted the last decade of her life to teaching and helping people in her community.

Also a missionary, she took a trip to Tanzania to evangelize and provide eyeglasses to those in need. She has organized various Bible studies in her hometown and currently is an active member of Christ the King Lutheran Church in Lambertville, Michigan.

Stacie is an avid hiker who has traveled to all fifty states. Her favorite vacation place is Sedona, Arizona, where she enjoys writing and hiking strenuous trails each year.

She currently resides in Toledo, Ohio.

For more information about

Stacie J. Ourlian

&

On The Edge

please visit
www.stacieourlian.com
www.twitter.com/StacieOurlian
ourlian@yahoo.com
www.facebook.com/staciejoourlian

For more information about
AMBASSADOR INTERNATIONAL
please visit:

www.ambassador-international.com
@AmbassadorIntl
www.facebook.com/AmbassadorIntl